MR. RHEE'S BRILLIANT MATH SERIES

PRACTICE TESTS FOR

I A A T

IOWA ALGEBRA APTITUDE TEST

VOLUME 2

by Brian Rhee

6 Additional
Full-Length Practice Tests

Detailed Solutions for All Questions

Legal Notice

IOWA Algebra Aptitude Test was not involved in the production of this publication nor endorses this book.

Copyright © 2017 by Solomon Academy
Published by: Solomon Academy
First Edition
ISBN-13: 978-1541393394
ISBN-10: 1541393392

Acknowledgements

I wish to acknowledge my deepest appreciation to my wife, Sookyung, who has continuously given me wholehearted support, encouragement, and love. Without you, I could not have completed this book.

Thank you to my sons, Joshua and Jason, who have given me big smiles and inspiration. I love you all.

About This Book

This book (Volume 2) is designed towards mastering the Iowa Algebra Aptitude Test (IAAT), a placement test which allows students to demonstrate their readiness and ability to succeed in Algebra 1. The book contains problems regarding essential theorems specific to the IAAT: Pre-Algebraic Number Skills and Concepts, Mathematical Data Interpretation and Analysis, Representing Relationships, and Symbols. There are 6 full-length math tests with detailed solutions and explanations for all questions.

Be sure to time yourself during the mathematic test with the appropriate time limit of 40 minutes. After completing any lessons or tests, immediately use the answer key and detailed solution to check your answers. Review all answers. Take the time to carefully read the explanations of problems you got incorrect. If you find yourself continually missing the same type of questions, look back at the topic summaries and review the theorems and examples in the lesson. Set a goal of improvement for each practice test.

About Author

Brian(Yeon) Rhee obtained a Masters of Arts Degree in Statistics at Columbia University, NY. He served as the Mathematical Statistician at the Bureau of Labor Statistics, DC. He is the Head Academic Director at Solomon Academy due to his devotion to the community coupled with his passion for teaching. His mission is to help students of all confidence level excel in academia to build a strong foundation in character, knowledge, and wisdom. Now, Solomon academy is known as the best academy specialized in Math in Northern Virginia.

Brian Rhee has published six books which are available in www.amazon.com. The titles of his books are AP Calculus, SAT 1 Math, SAT 2 Math level 2, SHSAT/TJHSST Math workbook, and IAAT, Volume 1(Iowa Algebra Aptitude Test) and IAAT, Volume 2. He's currently working on other math books which will be introduced in the near future.

Brian Rhee has twenty years of teaching experience in math. He has been one of the most popular tutors among TJHSST (Thomas Jefferson High School For Science and Technology) students. Currently, he is developing many online math courses with www.masterprep.net for AP Calculus AB and BC, SAT 2 Math level 2 test, and other various math subjects.

About IOWA Algebra Aptitude Test

The Iowa Algebra Aptitude Test (IAAT) is a placement test which allows students to demonstrate their readiness and ability to succeed in Algebra I. Students who pass with at least 91% percentile in the IAAT test will be granted the opportunity to take Algebra I in 7th grade. Notice that 91% percentile does not mean 91% correct; the score needed to quality for Algebra I differs each year.

The Iowa Algebra Aptitude Test (IAAT) is a timed test. Although the administered time is approximately 70 minutes, the actual test-taking time is 40 minutes. The IAAT consists of 60 questions divided into four subtests; each subtest will be allotted 10 minutes for completion.

Pre-Algebraic Number Skills and Concepts
This subtests measures the student's capability to solve mathematics problems, understand Pre-Algebraic concepts and basic computational skills: Whole Numbers, Fractions and Mixed Numbers, Decimals and Percents, Estimation, and Ratios.

Mathematical Data Interpretation and Analysis
This subtests measures the student's capability to learn new information presented in text or graphs.

Representing Relationships
The student must demonstrate the ability to find the formulas and rules of a given numerical relationship whether depicted verbally or in table.

Symbols
Students must understand important symbols of algebra and how to apply them. This subtest includes solving algebraic expression and applying symbolic representation.

Contents

IAAT Topic Summaries   9

Practice Test 1 Section 1   24

Practice Test 1 Section 2   27

Practice Test 1 Section 3   31

Practice Test 1 Section 4   35

Practice Test 1 Section 1 Answers and Solutions   38

Practice Test 1 Section 2 Answers and Solutions   40

Practice Test 1 Section 3 Answers and Solutions   42

Practice Test 1 Section 4 Answers and Solutions   45

Practice Test 2 Section 1   48

Practice Test 2 Section 2   51

Practice Test 2 Section 3   55

Practice Test 2 Section 4   58

Practice Test 2 Section 1 Answers and Solutions   61

Practice Test 2 Section 2 Answers and Solutions   64

Practice Test 2 Section 3 Answers and Solutions   66

Practice Test 2 Section 4 Answers and Solutions   68

Practice Test 3 Section 1   71

Practice Test 3 Section 2   74

Practice Test 3 Section 3   78

Practice Test 3 Section 4   82

Practice Test 3 Section 1 Answers and Solutions 85

Practice Test 3 Section 2 Answers and Solutions 88

Practice Test 3 Section 3 Answers and Solutions 90

Practice Test 3 Section 4 Answers and Solutions 93

Practice Test 4 Section 1 95

Practice Test 4 Section 2 98

Practice Test 4 Section 3 102

Practice Test 4 Section 4 106

Practice Test 4 Section 1 Answers and Solutions 109

Practice Test 4 Section 2 Answers and Solutions 111

Practice Test 4 Section 3 Answers and Solutions 113

Practice Test 4 Section 4 Answers and Solutions 116

Practice Test 5 Section 1 119

Practice Test 5 Section 2 122

Practice Test 5 Section 3 126

Practice Test 5 Section 4 130

Practice Test 5 Section 1 Answers and Solutions 133

Practice Test 5 Section 2 Answers and Solutions 135

Practice Test 5 Section 3 Answers and Solutions 137

Practice Test 5 Section 4 Answers and Solutions 140

Practice Test 6 Section 1 143

Practice Test 6 Section 2 146

Practice Test 6 Section 3 150

Practice Test 6 Section 4 153

Practice Test 6 Section 1 Answers and Solutions 156

Practice Test 6 Section 2 Answers and Solutions 159

Practice Test 6 Section 3 Answers and Solutions 161

Practice Test 6 Section 4 Answers and Solutions 163

IAAT TOPIC SUMMARIES

Factors

Factors are the numbers that you multiply to get another number. For instance, $10 = 1 \times 10$ and $10 = 2 \times 5$. Thus, the factors of 10 are 1, 2, 5, and 10.

Prime and Composite Numbers

A **prime number** is a whole number that has only two factors: 1 and itself. The prime numbers less than 60 are 2, 3, 5, 7, 11, 13, 17, 19, 23, 29, 31, 37, 41, 43, 47, 53, and 59. It is worth noting that 2 is the first, smallest, and only even prime number among the prime numbers. A **composite number** is a number that has more than two factors. For instance, 4 has three factors and is composite: 1, 2, and 4. 0 and 1 are neither prime nor composite.

Prime Factorization

A **prime factorization** of a number is the process of writing the number as the product of all its prime factors. Since 12 can be written as $12 = 2 \times 2 \times 3$, the prime factorization of 12 is $2^2 \times 3$.

Remainder

A **remainder**, r, is the amount left over when a number is divided by a divisor. For instance, when 7 is divided by 2, the quotient is 3 and the remainder is 1. The remainder must always be less than the divisor but greater than or equal to 0.

The Order of Operations

The order of operations is used to simplify or evaluate numerical expressions. The order of operations is depicted by the acronym, PEMDAS: P stands for parenthesis, E stands for exponent, M stands for multiplication, D stands for division, A stands for addition, and S stands for subtraction.

The order of operations suggests to first perform any calculations inside parentheses. Afterwards, evaluate any exponents. Next, perform all multiplications and divisions working from left to right. Finally, do additions and subtractions from left to right. The example below shows how to evaluate numerical expressions using PEMDAS.

$$12(3-4)^2 \div 4 - 2 = 12(-1)^2 \div 4 - 2$$
$$= 12 \div 4 - 2$$
$$= 3 - 2$$
$$= 1$$

Adding and Subtracting Decimals

When adding and subtracting numbers containing decimal places, write down the numbers vertically and line up decimal points. Place zeros into the numbers so that all numbers have the same number of decimal places. Then, proceed to evaluate. For example, $4.05 + 3.1 + 2.055 = 9.205$

$$
\begin{array}{r}
4.05 \\
3.1 \\
+ \quad 2.055 \\
\hline
9.205
\end{array}
$$

Multiplying Decimals

When multiplying numbers containing decimal points, multiply ignoring the decimal points. Afterwards, place a decimal point into the product same as the total number of decimal places the two factors have together. For instance, let's multiply 5×0.4. First, convert 5×0.4 into $5 \times 4 = 20$ by removing all decimal points. Since 5 has no decimal places and 0.4 has one number after the decimal point, the product of 5×0.4 will have one decimal place. Thus, $5 \times 0.4 = 2$.

Dividing Decimals

To divide decimals, it is necessary to convert the divisor, or the number you are dividing by, into a whole number. The number of decimal places that the decimal point moves in the divisor must be mirrored by the dividend. Proceed to use long division to evaluate and add a decimal point in the same spot as the dividend. For example, $25 \div 1.6 = 250 \div 16$. After you have converted the divisor into a whole number, it is possible to use long division; $25 \div 1.6 = 250 \div 16 = 15\frac{5}{8}$.

Fractions

A fraction is a number that represents a part of a whole; all parts are equal to each other. The top number is the numerator and the bottom number is the denominator. There are three types of fractions: Proper Fractions, Improper Fractions, and Mixed Fractions. Mixed Fractions are commonly referred to as Mixed Numbers. A Proper Fraction is defined when the numerator is less than the denominator. An Improper Fraction has a numerator that is greater than (or equal to) the denominator. A Mixed Fraction, or Mixed Number, consists of a whole number and a proper fraction together.

$$\text{Examples of Proper Fractions are } \frac{2}{3}, \frac{5}{11}, \frac{24}{25}$$

$$\text{Examples of Improper Fractions are } \frac{3}{2}, \frac{11}{5}, \frac{25}{24}, \frac{3}{3}$$

$$\text{Examples of Proper Fractions are } 1\frac{1}{2}, 2\frac{1}{5}, 1\frac{1}{25}$$

Simplifying Fractions

To simplify a fraction, divide the top and bottom by the greatest common factor, or by the highest number that can divide into both numbers exactly. In order to simplify $\frac{30}{54}$, it is necessary to find the greatest common factor, or GCF, of 30 and 54. To find the greatest common factor, it is possible to use two different methods: listing out all the factors of each number and comparing or prime factorization. The prime factorization method is different from the least common multiple; therefore, be aware and do **NOT** get them mixed up.

Factors of 30: 1, 2, 3, 5, **6**, 10, 15, 30
Factors of 54: 1, 2, 3, **6**, 9, 18, 27, 54
Since 6 is the largest common factor of 30 and 54, 6 is the GCF.

The prime factorization of 30: $2 \times 3 \times 5$
The prime factorization of 54: $2 \times 3 \times 3 \times 3$
To find the GCF from the prime factorization, multiply the terms that they have in common. Although 54 has three 3's, 30 only has one 3 so both 30 and 54 only have one 3 in common. Since both 30 and 54 have one 2 and one 3 in common, the GCF is the product of all common prime factors: $2 \times 3 = 6$.

After obtaining the greatest common factor, divide both the numerator and demoninator of the fraction by the GCF to obtain the simplest form.

$$\frac{30}{54} = \frac{30 \div 6}{54 \div 6} = \frac{5}{9}$$

Adding and Subtracting Fractions

When adding and subtracting fractions, it is necessary to have a common denominator. If the fractions have a common denominator, proceed to add. Only the numerator increases and decreases in value as the denominator stays the same because the denominator represents how many parts represent a whole. For example, $\frac{1}{4} + \frac{2}{4} = \frac{3}{4}$.

When adding and subtracting fractions with unlike denominators, it is necessary to find the least common denominator. The least common denominator is the least common multiple of the denominators which can be found by listing out the multiples for each number or by a prime factorization method. For example, evaluate $\frac{3}{24} + \frac{5}{56}$. Since the denominators are 24 and 56, let's find the least common multiple of 24 and 56.

Multiples of 24: 24, 48, 72, 96, 120, 144, **168**, 192, $\cdots$
Multiples of 56: 56, 112, **168**, 224, $\cdots$
Since 168 is the smallest common multiple of 24 and 56, 168 is the LCM.

The prime factorization of 24: $2 \times 2 \times 2 \times 3 = 2^3 \times 3$
The prime factorization of 56: $2 \times 2 \times 2 \times 7 = 2^3 \times 7$
Since the prime factors of both numbers consist of 2, 3, and 7, multiply the greatest power of 2, 3, and 7 that appear in either prime factorization. Since both numbers have 2^3, it doesn't matter and 2^3 is the greater factorization of 2. 3 only appears in the prime factorization of 24 and, likewise, 7 only appears in the prime factorization of 56. Therefore, the LCM of 24 and 56 is $2^3 \times 3 \times 7 = 168$.

Since the least common multiple is 168, it is necessary to convert each fraction to have a denominator of 168 by multiplying both the top and bottom by the same factor.

$$\frac{3}{24} = \frac{3 \times 7}{24 \times 7} = \frac{21}{168}$$

$$\frac{5}{56} = \frac{5 \times 3}{56 \times 3} = \frac{15}{168}$$

Thus, $\frac{3}{24} + \frac{5}{56} = \frac{21}{168} + \frac{15}{168} = \frac{36}{168}$. Since the greatest common factor of 36 and 168 is 12, $\frac{36}{168}$ simplifies to $\frac{3}{14}$.

Multiplying Fractions

To multiply fractions, multiply the numerators and then multiply the denominators. Simplify if necessary. It may be possible to cross simplify prior to multiplying.

$$\text{First Method:} \quad \frac{3}{4} \times \frac{2}{9} = \frac{3 \times 2}{4 \times 9} = \frac{6}{36} = \frac{1}{6}$$

$$\text{Second Method:} \quad \frac{3}{4} \times \frac{2}{9} = \frac{3}{9} \times \frac{2}{4} = \frac{1}{3} \times \frac{1}{2} = \frac{1}{6}$$

Dividing Fractions

To divide fractions, multiply by the reciprocal, or multiplicative inverse, of the divisor (second fraction). When you multiply a number by its respective multiplicative inverse, or reciprocal, the product is 1. For example, the reciprocal of 4 is $\frac{1}{4}$ because $4 \times \frac{1}{4} = 1$. Observe the example below. The divisor, or the number you are dividing by, is the second fraction $\frac{2}{7}$. Thus, multiply $\frac{1}{5}$ by the reciprocal of $\frac{2}{7}$. The reciprocal of $\frac{2}{7}$ is $\frac{7}{2}$.

$$\frac{1}{5} \div \frac{2}{7} = \frac{1}{5} \times \frac{7}{2} = \frac{7}{10}$$

Converting Fractions, Decimals, and Percentages

In order to **convert fractions into decimals**, simply divide. However, it is necessary to memorize some common fractions as depicted by the table below.

$\frac{1}{10} = 0.1$	$\frac{2}{10} = \frac{1}{5} = 0.2$	$\frac{3}{10} = 0.3$	$\frac{4}{10} = \frac{2}{5} = 0.4$	$\frac{5}{10} = \frac{1}{2} = 0.5$
$\frac{6}{10} = \frac{3}{5} = 0.6$	$\frac{7}{10} = 0.7$	$\frac{8}{10} = \frac{4}{5} = 0.8$	$\frac{9}{10} = 0.9$	$\frac{10}{10} = 1$

$\frac{1}{9} = 0.111\cdots = 0.\overline{1}$	$\frac{2}{9} = 0.222\cdots = 0.\overline{2}$	$\frac{3}{9} = 0.333\cdots = 0.\overline{3}$	$\frac{4}{9} = 0.444\cdots = 0.\overline{4}$
$\frac{5}{9} = 0.555\cdots = 0.\overline{5}$	$\frac{6}{9} = 0.666\cdots = 0.\overline{6}$	$\cdots$	$\frac{9}{9} = 1$

$\frac{1}{6} = 0.166\cdots = 0.1\overline{6}$	$\frac{2}{6} = \frac{1}{3} = 0.333\cdots = 0.\overline{3}$	$\frac{4}{6} = \frac{2}{3} = 0.666\cdots = 0.\overline{6}$	$\frac{5}{6} = 0.833\cdots = 0.8\overline{3}$

$\frac{1}{8} = 0.125$	$\frac{2}{8} = \frac{1}{4} = 0.25$	$\frac{3}{8} = 0.375$	$\frac{4}{8} = \frac{1}{2} = 0.5$
$\frac{5}{8} = 0.625$	$\frac{6}{8} = \frac{3}{4} = 0.75$	$\frac{7}{8} = 0.875$	$\frac{8}{8} = 1$

When **converting fractions into percentages**, attempt to set the denominator to 100 by multiplication. After multiplying both the numerator and denominator by the same factor, the numerator represents the percentage.

$$\frac{4}{25} = \frac{4 \times 4}{25 \times 4} = \frac{16}{100} = 16\%$$

If it is not possible to convert the denominator into 100 or deemed too complicated, convert the fraction into a decimal by dividing and then convert the decimal into percentage.

To **convert decimals into percentages**, multiply the number by 100 and add the % (percent) sign or move the decimal point two places to the right. In order to **convert percentages into decimals**, divide the number by 100 and remove the % (percent) sign or move the decimal point two places to the left.

Integers

Natural numbers are positive counting numbers starting from one: $1, 2, 3, \cdots, +\infty$. **Whole numbers** are counting numbers including zero: $0, 1, 2, \cdots, +\infty$. A hint to remember that whole numbers include zero is that the word "whole" has the letter o which looks like the number zero, 0. **Integers** are counting numbers which include zero, and negative and positive numbers: $-\infty, \cdots, -2, -1, 0, 1, 2, \cdots, +\infty$.

Since integers consist of both positive and negative numbers, there are different rules when performing the four operations: adding, subtracting, multiplying, and dividing. When evaluating an expression, use the **order of operations (PEMDAS)**. The order of operations suggests to first perform any calculations inside parentheses. Afterwards, evaluate any exponents. Next, perform all multiplications and divisions working from left to right. Finally, do additions and subtractions from left to right.

When **adding integers**, you must take into consideration the magnitude of the positive and negative values. When adding two positive integers, the sum becomes more positive. Likewise, when adding two negative integers, the sum becomes more negative. Let's use a common metaphor which relates positive and negative values. Think of positive integers as good guys and negative integers as bad guys. Good guys plus good guys will equal even more good guys. Likewise, bad guys plus bad guys result in even more bad guys. When adding a positive integer and a negative integer, compare to see which of the following has more value. For example, 5 good guys verses 2 bad guys will result in a win for the good guys because there are 3 more good guys. Thus, when adding $5 + (-2)$, the sum is positive 3. On the other hand, if 5 bad guys verses 2 good guys, the bad guys will win because they have a stronger pull by 3 bad guys. Since there are 3 bad guys remaining and bad guys are negative, when adding $-5 + 2$, the sum is -3. The metaphor, although simple, proves the theory of adding integers. Be careful and pay close attention to which number, positive or negative, has a larger impact.

Another concept to understand is that adding a negative is the same concept as subtracting. Let's use $6 + (-4)$ for example. Since adding a negative means subtraction, $6 + (-4)$ can be rewritten as $6 - 4 = 2$. Even if the question was originally written $(-4) + 6$, it is possible to use the commutative property of addition to rewrite it as $6 + (-4)$.

$$6 + 4 = 10 \qquad \text{(Adding two positive integers)}$$
$$-7 + (-5) = -12 \qquad \text{(Adding two negative integers)}$$
$$7 + (-18) = -11 \qquad \text{(Adding a positive and negative integer)}$$
$$(-4) + 7 = 3 \qquad \text{(Adding a positive and negative integer)}$$

Pay close attention when **subtracting integers**. When subtracting integers, picture a number line. For example, let's take the problem $6 - 8$. Since 6 is positive, walk 6 steps right from the starting position. Afterwards, since you are subtracting 8 from the new location, walk left 8 spaces and you will be 2 spaces left from the starting position. Thus, $6 - 8 = -2$. The only tricky aspect of subtracting integers is when subtracting a negative number. In the example, $-4 - (-8)$, we start off by walking 4 steps left from the starting position. Although subtracting indicates walking left, subtracting a negative reverses the walking direction and instead you must walk 8 steps to the right. In other words, subtracting a negative number means to add. Therefore, $-4 - (-8)$ can be rewritten as $-4 + 8$ which equals positive 4. Adding and subtracting integers can be placed into two rules. When two like signs are adjacent to each other, it means to add. When two unlike signs are adjacent to each other, it means to subtract.

In order to **multiply integers**, the number of the product will be the same but it is necessary to observe whether or not the number is positive or negative. When multiplying two like signs together, the answer is always positive: $+ \times + = +$ and $- \times - = +$. When multiplying a positive and negative number, the product is always negative: $+ \times - = -$ and $- \times + = -$. When an expression has only multiplication, it is possible to determine whether or not the product is positive or negative by counting the number of negative terms. If the expression has an even number of negative values, the product will be positive. However, if the expression consists of an odd number of negative values, the product will be negative. It is also possible to take each term in the expression step by step. For example, $-4 \times 4 \times (-4) = -16 \times (-4) = +64$.

$$5 \times 4 = 20 \quad \text{(Multiplying two positive integers)}$$
$$-5 \times (-4) = 20 \quad \text{(Multiplying two negative integers)}$$
$$-5 \times 4 = -20 \quad \text{(Multiplying a positive and negative integer)}$$
$$5 \times (-4) = -20 \quad \text{(Multiplying a positive and negative integer)}$$

$$2 \times (-2) \times (-2) \times (-2) \times (-2) = 32 \quad \text{(Product is positive because even number of negative integers)}$$
$$2 \times (-2) \times (-2) \times (-2) \times 2 = -32 \quad \text{(Product is negative because odd number of negative integers)}$$

Dividing integers follow the same rules as multiplying integers. When dividing two like signs together, the answer is always positive: $+ \div + = +$ and $- \div - = +$. When dividing a positive and negative number, the quotient is always negative: $+ \div - = -$ and $- \div + = -$.

$$20 \div 5 = 4 \quad \text{(Dividing two positive integers)}$$
$$-20 \div (-5) = 4 \quad \text{(Dividing two negative integers)}$$
$$-20 \div 5 = -4 \quad \text{(Dividing a positive and negative integer)}$$
$$20 \div (-5) = -4 \quad \text{(Dividing a positive and negative integer)}$$

Algebraic Properties

Commutative Property of Addition: The order in which numbers are added in an expression does not change the sum: $x + y = y + x$.

$$5 + 4 = 4 + 5$$
$$9 = 9$$

Commutative Property of Multiplication: The order in which numbers are multiplied in an expression does not change the product: $x \cdot y = y \cdot x$.

$$5 \times 4 = 4 \times 5$$
$$20 = 20$$

Associative Property of Addition: When adding, the order and way in which numbers are grouped does not change the sum: $(x + y) + z = x + (y + z)$.

$$(3 + 4) + 5 = 3 + (4 + 5)$$
$$7 + 5 = 3 + 9$$
$$12 = 12$$

Associative Property of Multiplication: When multiplying, the order and way in which numbers are grouped does not change the product: $(x \times y) \times z = x \times (y \times z)$.

$$(3 \cdot 4) \cdot 5 = 3 \cdot (4 \cdot 5)$$
$$12 \cdot 5 = 3 \cdot 20$$
$$60 = 60$$

Additive Identity: When adding 0 to any number, the sum is the number: $x + 0 = x$.

$$-10 + 0 = -10$$

Multiplicative Identity: When multiplying 1 to any number, the product is the number: $x \cdot 1 = x$.

$$-10 \cdot 1 = -10$$

Multiplicative Property of Zero: When multiplying 0 to any number, the product is zero: $x \cdot 0 = 0$.

$$-10 \cdot 0 = 0$$

Symmetric Property: If one measure equals a second measure, then the second measure equals the first: if $a = b$, then $b = a$.

$$\text{If } 4 + 3 = 7, \text{ then } 7 = 4 + 3.$$

Transitive Property: If one measure equals a second measure and the second measure equals a third measure, then the first measure equals the third measure: if $a = b$ and $b = c$, then $a = c$.

$$\text{If } 2 + 7 = 3 \times 3 \text{ and } 3 \times 3 = 9, \text{ then } 2 + 7 = 9.$$

Distributive Property: The distributive property demonstrates multiplying a number by a sum. In other words, multiply each number inside a parenthesis by the number outside of the parenthesis. When evaluating expressions, it is necessary to solve expressions inside the parentheses first; however, the distributive property is necessary when dealing with variables inside the parenthesis.

$$2(3 + 5) = 2(3) + 2(5)$$

As illustrated in the example above, the 2 is distributed to the 3 and then the 2 is distributed to the 5. Afterwards, proceed to multiply and add.

$$2(3) + 2(5) = 6 + 10 = 16$$

The number you are multiplying by can be written outside of the parenthesis either on the left or right side: $a(b + c)$ or $(b + c)a$. Both are correct; however, $a(b + c)$ is more commonly represented in algebraic problems. It is necessary to understand how negative numbers are distributed. For example, $10 - (2 + 3)$ is not the same as $10 - 2 + 3$. The negative sign must be distributed into both terms inside the parenthesis: $10 - 2 - 3$. Likewise, when dealing with negative numbers, the negative must be distributed into each term within the parenthesis. The eight examples below represent the different possible outcomes when multiplying a term and a binomial.

$$a(b + c) = ab + ac$$
$$a(b - c) = ab - ac$$
$$a(-b + c) = -ab + ac$$
$$a(-b - c) = -ab - ac$$
$$-a(b + c) = -ab - ac$$
$$-a(b - c) = -ab + ac$$
$$-a(-b + c) = ab - ac$$
$$-a(-b - c) = ab + ac$$

Variables

Variables are letters that act as an unknown in a problem and are depicted by a variety of letters including, but not limited to, x, y, and n. In simple terms, observe the equation $x + 2 = 5$. Since $3 + 2 = 5$, the variable x is equal to 3 as it serves as a placeholder and unknown in the problem.

Combining Like Terms

Like terms are terms that have same variables and same exponent; only the coefficients may be different but can be the same. Knowing like terms is essential when you simplify algebraic expressions. For instance,

- $2x$ and $3x$: (Like terms)

- $2x$ and $3x^2$: (Not like terms since the two expressions have different exponents)

- 2 and 3: (Like terms)

To simplify algebraic expressions, expand the expression using the distributive property when necessary. Then group the like terms and simplify them. For instance,

$$
\begin{aligned}
2(-x + 2) + 3x + 5 &= -2x + 4 + 3x + 5 \qquad \text{(Use distributive property to expand)} \\
&= (-2x + 3x) + (4 + 5) \qquad \text{(Group the like terms and simplify)} \\
&= x + 9
\end{aligned}
$$

To evaluate an algebraic expression, substitute the numerical value into the variable. When substituting a negative numerical value, make sure to use a **parenthesis** to avoid a mistake.

Solving Equations and Word Problems

Solving an equation is finding the value of the variable that makes the equation true. In order to solve an equation, use the rule called SADMEP with inverse operations (SADMEP is the reverse order of the order of operations, PEMDAS). Inverse operations are the operations that cancel each other. Addition and subtraction, and multiplication and division are good examples.

SADMEP suggests to first cancel subtraction or addition. Then, cancel division or multiplication next by applying corresponding inverse operation. Below is an example that shows you how to solve $2x - 1 = 5$, which involves subtraction and multiplication.

$$
\begin{aligned}
2x - 1 &= 5 \\
+1 &= +1 \\
2x &= 6 \\
x &= 3
\end{aligned}
$$

$$\checkmark \quad \checkmark$$
$$S\ A\ D\ M\ E\ P$$

Addition to cancel substraction

Division to cancel multiplication

Solving word problems involve translating verbal phrases into mathematical equations. The table below summarizes the guidelines.

Verbal Phrase	Expression
A number	x
Is	$=$
Of	$\times$
Percent	0.01 or $\frac{1}{100}$
The sum of x and y	$x + y$
Three more than twice a number	$2x + 3$
The difference of x and y	$x - y$
3 is subtracted from a number	$x - 3$
4 less than a number	$x - 4$
A number decreased by 5	$x - 5$
6 less a number	$6 - x$
The product of x and y	xy
6 times a number	$6x$
The quotient of x and y	$\frac{x}{y}$
A number divided by 9	$\frac{x}{9}$

For instance, use SADMEP to solve for x in the verbal phrase: 5 more than the quotient of x and 3 is 14.

$$
\begin{aligned}
&\checkmark\ \checkmark \\
\frac{x}{3} + 5 = 14 \qquad & S\ A\ D\ M\ E\ P \\
-5 = -5 \qquad & \text{Subtraction to cancel addition} \\
\frac{x}{3} = 9 \qquad & \text{Multiplication to cancel division} \\
x = 27 \qquad &
\end{aligned}
$$

Solving Inequalities

Solving an inequality is exactly the same as solving an equation. To solve an inequality, use SADMEP (Reverse order of the PEMDAS). In most cases, the inequality symbol remains unchanged. However, there are only two cases in which the inequality symbol must be reversed. The first case is when you multiply or divide each side by a negative number. The second case is when you take a reciprocal of each side. For instance,

<table>
<tr><td align="center">Case 1</td><td align="center">Case 2</td></tr>
<tr><td align="center">$2 < 3$</td><td align="center">$2 < 3$</td></tr>
<tr><td align="center">$-2 > -3$</td><td align="center">$\dfrac{1}{2} > \dfrac{1}{3}$</td></tr>
</table>

For instance, use SADMEP to solve the inequality $-3x + 2 > x + 10$.

$$-3x + 2 > x + 10 \qquad \text{Subtract } x \text{ from each side}$$
$$-4x + 2 > 10 \qquad \text{Subtract 2 from each side}$$
$$-4x > 8 \qquad \text{Divide each side by } -4$$
$$x < -2 \qquad \text{Reverse the inequality symbol}$$

Ratios, Rates, and Proportions

A **ratio** is a fraction that compares two quantities measured in the same units. The ratio of a to b can be written as $a : b$ or $\frac{a}{b}$. If the ratio of a number of apples to that of oranges in a store is $3 : 4$ or $\frac{3}{4}$, it means that there are 3 apples to every 4 oranges in the store.

A **rate** is a ratio that compares two quantities measured in different units. A rate is usually expressed as a unit rate. A unit rate is a rate per one unit of a given quantity. The rate of a per b can be written as $\frac{a}{b}$. If a car travels 100 miles in 2 hours, the car travels at a rate of 50 miles per hour.

A **proportions** is an equation that states that two ratios are equal A proportion can be written as

$$a : b = c : d \quad \text{or} \quad \frac{a}{b} = \frac{c}{d}$$

The proportion above reads a is to b as c is to d. To solve the value of a variable in a proportion, use the cross product property and then solve for the variable. For instance,

$$\frac{x}{2} = \frac{6}{3} \qquad \text{Cross Product Property}$$
$$3x = 2 \times 6$$
$$x = 4$$

Properties of Exponents

In the expression 2^4, 2 is the base, 4 is the exponent, and 2^4 is the power. Exponents represent how many times the base is multiplied by. $2^4 = 2 \times 2 \times 2 \times 2$. The table below shows a summary of the properties of exponents .

Properties of Exponents	Example
1. $a^m \cdot a^n = a^{m+n}$	1. $2^4 \cdot 2^6 = 2^{10}$
2. $\frac{a^m}{a^n} = a^{m-n}$	2. $\frac{2^{10}}{2^3} = 2^{10-3} = 2^7$
3. $a^0 = 1$	4. $(-2)^0 = 1, (3)^0 = 1, (100)^0 = 1$
4. $a^{-1} = \frac{1}{a}$	5. $2^{-1} = \frac{1}{2}$

Scientific Notation

Scientific notation is the process of writing large or small numbers in the form of $c \times 10^n$ where $1 \leq c < 10$ and n is an integer. In other words, c must be greater than or equal to 1 but less than 10. In general, positive n values give a large number while negative n values produce small fractional values. It is important to understand how to convert numbers written in standard notation to scientific notation and vice versa.

To **convert standard notation to scientific notation**, set the decimal point to create a number that satisfies the definition of c. For example, the c value of 12,400 is 1.24. Since 12,400 is a large number and the decimal point moved 4 places to the left, the scientific notation is written as $12,400 = 1.24 \times 10,000 = 1.24 \times 10^4$. For smaller numbers such as 0.000000024, the c value is 2.4. Since the number is small and the decimal point moved 8 places to the right, the scientific notation is written as $0.000000024 = \frac{2.4}{100,000,000} = 2.4 \times 10^{-8}$

Functions and Relations

An ordered pair (x, y) describes the location of a point on the coordinate system. The first number in the ordered pair describes the x-coordinate, or the position relevant to the x-axis. The x-coordinate is often referred to as the **input** and the set of all x-values in a given set is called the **domain**. The second number in the ordered pair describes the y-coordinate, or the position relevant to the y-axis. The y-coordinate is often referred to as the **output** and the set of all y-values in a given set is called the **range**. A set of ordered pairs is described as a **relation**. A relation can be depicted in several ways.

$$\{(1, 2), (2, 3), (3, 4), (4, 5)\}$$

x	1	2	3	4
y	2	3	4	5

x	y
1	2
2	3
3	4
4	5

A **function** is a special type of relation that relates a specific input to exactly one output. Each member of the domain, or x-value, is paired with only one member of the range, or y-value. The x-value cannot repeat nor have multiple y-coordinates. The y-value can repeat. In other words, a function relates an input to an output so that an input x cannot have more than one value for an output y. For instance, let's consider the following scenario. On Monday, you make 10 dollars. Is it, then, possible to make 10 dollars again on Tuesday? Sure it is. There is nothing stopping you from making the same about of money you did on the previous day. This shows the concept of how the y-coordinate can repeat which represents the dollars earned in a given day of the week. However, this next statement shows ambiguity and is unclear on what it is trying to display. On Monday, you make 10 dollars. On Monday, you make 5 dollars. Did you make 5 dollars or 10 dollars on Monday. If you made 15 dollars, why didn't you state, "On Monday, I made 15 dollars." This is an example of why a function defines a relation that every member of the domain is paired with exactly one member of its range. If you made 5 dollars on the Monday of Week 1 and 10 dollars on the Monday of Week 2, then those are two separate x-coordinate values: $(\text{Mon}_1, 5), (\text{Mon}_2, 10)$.

When illustrated as a graph or scatter plot, it is possible to determine whether or not the shown relation is a function or not. Use the **vertical line test**. If, at any position on the graph, a vertical line can be drawn that passes through two different points, the relation fails the vertical line test and is **NOT** a function.

A function can be described using a symbol. For example, $a \odot b = \frac{2a}{b}$. The symbol, $\odot$, represents the expression $\frac{2a}{b}$ as where a and b are both variables. Thus, if a and b are given, it is possible to evaluate the expression. If $a \odot b = \frac{2a}{b}$, what is $3 \odot 9$?

$$a \odot b = \frac{2a}{b}$$

$$3 \odot 9 = \frac{2(3)}{9} = \frac{6}{9} = \frac{2}{3}$$

Linear Equations

The **slope**, m, of a line is a number that describes the steepness of the line. If a line passes through the points (x_1, y_1) and (x_2, y_2), the slope m is defined as

$$m = \frac{\text{Rise}}{\text{Run}} = \frac{y_2 - y_1}{x_2 - x_1}$$

An equation of a line can be written in slope-intercept form, $y = mx + b$, where m is slope and b is y-intercept. Below classifies the lines by slope.

- Lines that rise from left to right have positive slope.

- Lines that fall from left to right have negative slope.

- Horizontal lines have zero slope (example: $y = 2$).

- Vertical lines have undefined slope (example: $x = 2$).

- Parallel lines have the same slope.

The x-**intercept** of a line is a point where the line crosses x-axis. The y-**intercept** of a line is a point where the line crosses y-axis.

To find the x-intercept of a line	$\Longrightarrow$	Substitute 0 for y and solve for x
To find the y-intercept of a line	$\Longrightarrow$	Substitute 0 for x and solve for y

IAAT PRACTICE TEST 1

SECTION 1
Time — 10 minutes
15 Questions

Directions: Read the information given and choose the best answer for each question. Base your answer only on the information given. The time limit for each section is 10 minutes.

1. Round 4563 to the nearest hundred.

   (A)   5000

   (B)   4600

   (C)   4560

   (D)   4000

2. Simplify $\frac{1}{2} + \frac{1}{3}$.

   (J) $\frac{5}{6}$

   (K) $\frac{3}{4}$

   (L) $\frac{2}{3}$

   (M) $\frac{1}{5}$

3. $12 + 123 + 1234 =$

   (A)   3664

   (B)   2589

   (C)   1477

   (D)   1369

4. If Mr. Rhee travels 108 miles in 3 hours, how many miles can he travel in 1 hour?

   (J)   36 miles

   (K)   54 miles

   (L)   108 miles

   (M)   162 miles

5. $13.2 \div 0.3 =$

   (A)   440

   (B)   44

   (C)   4.4

   (D)   0.44

6. Which of the following number CANNOT divide 96 by?

   (J)   6

   (K)   8

   (L)   12

   (M)   13

7. $4.6 \times 7.4 =$

    (A)   34.04

    (B)   33.84

    (C)   32.14

    (D)   31.64

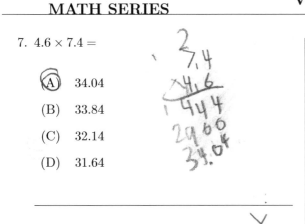

8. The lengths of two squares are 2, and 3, respectively. What is the ratio of the area of the smaller square to that of the larger square?

    (J) $1 : 2$

    (K) $2 : 3$

    (L) $3 : 5$

    (M) $4 : 9$

9. Which of the following expression has the largest value?

    (A) $-4 + 2$

    (B) -4×2

    (C) $(-4)^2$

    (D) $-\frac{1}{4}$

10. $5 - 2(1 - 3 - 5) =$

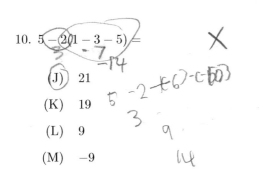

    (J)   21

    (K)   19

    (L)   9

    (M) -9

11. Which of the following fraction is the same as 0.875 ?

    (A) $\frac{11}{10}$

    (B) $\frac{9}{10}$

    (C) $\frac{7}{8}$

    (D) $\frac{4}{5}$

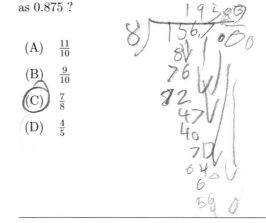

12. The original cost of a jacket was \$45. If Jason bought it at 40% off, how much did he save?

    (J)   18

    (K)   24

    (L)   27

    (M)   32

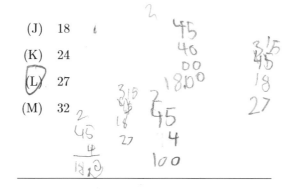

13. $\sqrt{196} =$

    (A)   12

    (B)   13

    (C)   14

    (D)   15

14. Joshua studied 10 hours last week. If he studied $\frac{1}{4}$ of the study time on math, how many hours and minutes did he spend on math?

    (J)   2 hours and 15 minutes

    (K)   2 hours and 30 minutes

    (L)   2 hours and 40 minutes

    (M)   2 hours and 50 minutes

15. Which of the following expression is equal to $2^2 \times 5^2$?

    (A) 10^2

    (B) 10^3

    (C) 10^4

    (D) 10^5

STOP

IAAT PRACTICE TEST 1

SECTION 2
Time — 10 minutes
15 Questions

Directions: Read the information given and choose the best answer for each question. Base your answer only on the information given. The time limit for each section is 10 minutes.

Directions: Use the following table to answer questions 1 − 4.

Solomon High School Athlete Participation

Sport	Number of Athletes
Swimming	58
Baseball	52
Basketball	48
Tennis	42

1. What is the total number of athletes in Solomon high school?

   (A) 180

   (B) 190

   (C) 200

   (D) 210

2. What is the median number of athletes participating in a sport?

   (J) 48

   (K) 49

   (L) 50

   (M) 52

3. What percentage of Solomon high school athletes participated in baseball?

   (A) 20%

   (B) 26%

   (C) 40%

   (D) 52%

4. According to the table, what is the probability that an athlete chosen at random participates in swimming?

   (J) 0.29

   (K) 0.36

   (L) 0.48

   (M) 0.58

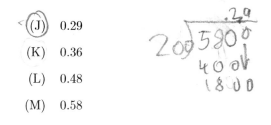

Directions: The following table shows different lunch choices. A lunch consists of 1 vegetable, 1 main dish, and 1 drink. Use the table to answer questions 5 – 8.

Lunch Choices

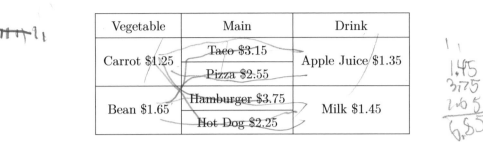

Vegetable	Main	Drink
Carrot $1.25	Taco $3.15	Apple Juice $1.35
	Pizza $2.55	
Bean $1.65	Hamburger $3.75	Milk $1.45
	Hot Dog $2.25	

5. How many different lunches are possible?

(A) 20

(B) 16

(C) 12

(D) 8

6. How much is a lunch consisting of 1 carrot, 1 taco, and 1 apple juice?

(J) $7.25

(K) $6.55

(L) $6.15

(M) $5.75

7. What is the amount of the cheapest lunch?

(A) $5.35

(B) $5.05

(C) $4.85

(D) $4.65

8. What is the amount of the most expensive lunch?

(J) $5.75

(K) $6.15

(L) $6.85

(M) $7.45

Directions: A survey asks all 6th graders in an elementary school which type of movie they are going to watch in a movie theatre. Use the following pie chart to answer questions 9 – 10.

Favorite Type of Movie

9. What is the total number of the 6th graders in the elementary school?

(A) 95

(B) 95

(C) 100

(D) 105

10. Which movie had twice as many as 6th graders as comedy?

(J) Drama

(K) Action

(L) Romance

(M) Cannot be determined

Column 1	Column 2	Column 3	Column 4
	1	2	3
4	5	6	7
8	9	10	11
⋮	⋮	⋮	⋮

11. If the pattern continues as shown above, which Column is 26 located?

(A) Column 1

(B) Column 2

(C) Column 3

(D) Column 4

M	T	W	R	F	Total
3.6	4.5	3.2	4.4		20

12. The table above shows the distance, in miles, that Mr. Rhee ran each day. If the total distance that Mr. Rhee ran is 20 miles, how many miles Mr. Rhee ran on Friday?

(J) 4.6

(K) 4.5

(L) 4.4

(M) 4.3

Directions: In the schedule below, each period is 45 minutes long, and each break is 10 minutes long. The first period begins at 8:30 AM. Use the following table to answer questions 13 − 15.

	Beginning Time	Ending Time
Period 1	8:30 AM	9:15
Break	9:15	9:25
Period 2	9:25	10:10
Break	10:15	10:25
Period 3	10:25	11:15

13. What time does the first period end?

(A) 9:15 AM

(B) 9:20 AM

(C) 9:25 AM

(D) 9:30 AM

14. What time does the 3rd period begin?

(J) 10:20 AM

(K) 10:25 AM

(L) 10:30 AM

(M) 10:35 AM

15. If lunch begins after the 3rd period and is hour long, what time does the lunch end?

(A) 12:05 PM

(B) 12:10 PM

(C) 12:15 PM

(D) 12:20 PM

STOP

IAAT PRACTICE TEST 1

SECTION 3

Time — 10 minutes

15 Questions

Directions: Read the information given and choose the best answer for each question. Base your answer only on the information given. The time limit for each section is 10 minutes.

1. Which of the following represents the next number in the sequence shown below?

$$81, 27, 9, 3, 1, \cdots$$

   (A) -1

   (B) 0

   (C) $\frac{1}{2}$

   (D) $\frac{1}{3}$

2. When $x = 2$, what is the value of y if $2x + 3y = 19$?

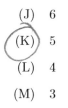

   (J)   6

   (K)   5

   (L)   4

   (M)   3

y	5	6	7
x	3	4	5

3. The table above shows three pairs of x and y values. Which of the following equation is true for all values in the table?

   (A) $y = x - 2$

   (B) $y = x + 2$

   (C) $y = 2x$

   (D) $y = 2x - 1$

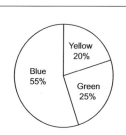

4. As shown above, students are divided into three groups: yellow team, green team, and blue team. Let T be the total number of students. Which of the following expression represents the number of students in the blue team?

   (J) $0.55T$

   (K) $55T$

   (L) $T + 0.55$

   (M) $T + 55$

5. Joshua is 15 years old now. Which of the following represents Joshua's age m years ago?

   (A) $m + 15$

   (B) $m - 15$

   (C) $15 - m$

   (D) $15m$

6. The area of a triangle is 14. If the base of the triangle is 14, what is the height of the triangle?

   (J)   6

   (K)   4

   (L)   2

   (M)   1

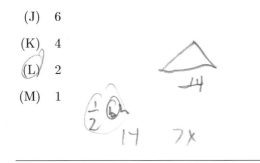

7. Which of the following equation best represents the following verbal relationship? The quotient of x and y is 10.

   (A) $x - y = 10$

   (B) $xy = 10$

   (C) $\frac{y}{x} = 10$

   (D) $\frac{x}{y} = 10$

Input	Output
1	2
2	5
3	8
⋮	⋮
6	17

8. Observe the numbers in the two columns shown above. Which of the following value should be in the empty cell?

   (J)   9

   (K)   8

   (L)   7

   (M)   6

9. Which of the following table contains only ordered pairs that satisfy the equation, $y = \frac{1}{2}x + 1$?

(A)

x	-2	0	2	4
y	0	2	3	4

(B)

x	-2	0	2	4
y	0	1	2	3

(C)

x	-2	0	2	4
y	-1	0	1	2

(D)

x	-2	0	2	4
y	-2	-1	0	1

Luggage Type	Number	Weight
Backpack	2	15 pounds/each
Suitcase	3	25 pounds/each

10. According to the table above, what is the total weight of the luggage in pounds?

   (J)   135 pounds

   (K)   125 pounds

   (L)   115 pounds

   (M)   105 pounds

11. If $A = -1$, $B = 3$, and $C = -2$, which of the following inequality best represents the relationship between A, B, and C ?

   (A) $A < B < C$

   (B) $B < A < C$

   (C) $C < A < B$

   (D) $C < B < A$

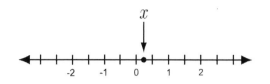

12. As shown above, x is on the number line. Which of the following value represents the value of x ?

   (J)   0.75

   (K)   0.25

   (L) -0.25

   (M) -0.75

13. Which of the following table best represents the following verbal relationship? The number of pens sold, y, is three less than half the number of pencils sold, x.

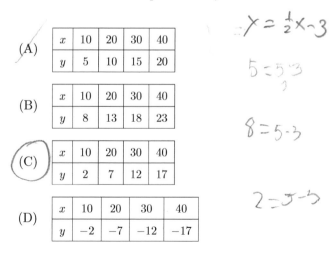

14. Joshua studied two hours a day for five days. What is the total number of hours that Joshua studied for the five days?

    (J)   20 hours

    (K)   15 hours

    (L)   10 hours

    (M)   5 hours

15. Jason and other students line up in a row to get lunch. Jason is the 5th from the front and 6th from the back. How many students including Jason in the line?

    (A)   10

    (B)   11

    (C)   12

    (D)   13

STOP

IAAT PRACTICE TEST 1
SECTION 4
Time — 10 minutes
15 Questions

Directions: Read the information given and choose the best answer for each question. Base your answer only on the information given. The time limit for each section is 10 minutes.

72 is 60 percent of a number, x

1. Which of the following equation represents the verbal phrase above?

   (A) $0.6x = 72$

   (B) $x + 0.6 = 72$

   (C) $\frac{x}{72} = 0.6$

   (D) $\frac{x}{0.6} = \frac{72}{100}$

2. Which of the following inequality has a solution of $x < -1$?

   (J) $x + 1 > 0$

   (K) $x - 3 < -2$

   (L) $-2x > 2$

   (M) $2x + 1 > -1$

3. If $a \clubsuit b = 2a + 3b$, what is the value of $3 \clubsuit 2$?

   (A) 12

   (B) 13

   (C) 14

   (D) 15

4. If $x = y + 7$, what is the value of $x - y$?

   (J) 1

   (K) 3

   (L) 7

   (M) 11

5. A tulip grows 2 inches in a week. Which proportion can be used to find x, the number of weeks needed for the tulip to grow 6 inches?

   (A) $\frac{1}{2} = \frac{6}{x}$

   (B) $\frac{2}{1} = \frac{6}{x}$

   (C) $\frac{2}{7} = \frac{6}{x}$

   (D) $\frac{7}{2} = \frac{6}{x}$

6. Solve for x: $4(x + 1) - 3 = 17$

   (J)   2

   (K)   3

   (L)   4

   (M)   5

7. Joshua can brew c cups of coffee with one ounce of ground coffee. How many cups can Joshua brew with four ounces of ground coffee?

   (A) $c + 4$ cups

   (B) $\frac{c}{4}$ cups

   (C) $\frac{4}{c}$ cups

   (D) $4c$ cups

8. Which phrase is represented by $2(x + y) = 4$?

   (J)   Two more than the sum of x and y is 4.

   (K)   Twice the quotient of x and y is 4.

   (L)   Two more than the product of x and y is 4.

   (M)   Twice the sum of x and y is 4.

9. Simplify the expression $\frac{3}{2}x + y + \frac{5}{2}x - 2y$.

   (A) $4x - y$

   (B) $4x + y$

   (C) $4 + 2x - y$

   (D) $4 + 2x + y$

10. If $5x = 6y$ and $y = 20$, what is the value of x ?

   (J)   12

   (K)   18

   (L)   24

   (M)   30

11. The area of a trapezoid is defined as $A = \frac{1}{2}(b_1 + b_2)h$, where b_1 and b_2 are the lengths of each base, and h is the height. If the lengths of each bases are 5 and 7, and the height is 6, what is the area of a trapezoid?

   (A)   24

   (B)   36

   (C)   48

   (D)   72

12. If $x = 2$ and $y = 8$, what is the value of $\sqrt{xy}$?

   (J)   4

   (K)   6

   (L)   8

   (M)   10

13. $-5(x - 2y) =$

$-5x^{-60y}$

(A) $-5x - 2y$

(B) $-5x + 2y$

(C) $10y - 5x$

(D) $10y + x$

15. Let $S(x)$ be the sum of all the positive integers less than or equal to x. For example, $S(5) = 1 + 2 + 3 + 4 + 5 = 15$. What is the value of $S(7)$?

(A) 26

(B) 27

(C) 28

(D) 29

14. If the perimeter of a square is $4x$, what is the area of the square in terms of x ?

(J) x^4

(K) x^2

(L) $4x$

(M) x

STOP

Answers and Solutions
IAAT Practice Test 1 Section 1

Answers

1. B	2. J	3. D	4. J	5. B
6. M	7. A	8. M	9. C	10. K
11. C	12. J	13. C	14. K	15. A

Solutions

1. (B)

   Rounding 4563 to the nearest hundred gives 4600. Therefore, (B) is the correct answer.

2. (J)

$$\frac{1}{2} + \frac{1}{3} = \frac{3}{6} + \frac{2}{6} = \frac{5}{6}$$

   Therefore, (J) is the correct answer.

3. (D)

   $12 + 123 + 1234 = 1369$. Therefore, (D) is the correct answer.

4. (J)

   If Mr. Rhee travels 108 miles in 3 hours, the number of miles that he can travel in 1 hour is $\frac{108}{3} = 36$. Therefore, (J) is the correct answer.

5. (B)

$$\frac{13.2}{0.3} = \frac{132}{3} = 44$$

   Therefore, (B) is the correct answer.

6. (M)

   If 96 is divided by 13, the remainder is 5. Therefore, (M) is the correct answer.

7. (A)

   $4.6 \times 7.4 = 34.04$. Therefore, (A) is the correct answer.

8. (M)

The area of the smaller square is $2^2 = 4$. The area of the larger square is $3^2 = 9$. Thus, the ratio of the area of the smaller square to that of the larger square is $4 : 9$. Therefore, (M) is the correct answer.

9. (C)

$(-4)^2 = 16$ is the largest value among answer choices. Therefore, (C) is the correct answer.

10. (K)

$$5 - 2(1 - 3 - 5) = 5 - 2(-7)$$
$$= 5 + 14$$
$$= 19$$

Therefore, (K) is the correct answer.

11. (C)

$\dfrac{11}{10} = 1.1$, $\dfrac{9}{10} = 0.9$, $\dfrac{7}{8} = 0.875$, and $\dfrac{4}{5} = 0.8$. Therefore, (C) is the correct answer.

12. (J)

The original cost of a jacket was $45. Jason bought it at 40% off. Thus, the amount that he saved was $0.4 \times \$45 = \$18$. Therefore, (J) is the correct answer.

13. (C)

Since $14^2 = 196$, $\sqrt{196} = 14$. Therefore, (C) is the correct answer.

14. (K)

Joshua studied $\frac{1}{4} \times 10$ hours or 2.5 hours hours on math. Since 0.5 hour is equal to 0.5×60 minutes $= 30$ minutes, 2.5 hours is equal to 2 hours and 30 minutes. Therefore, (K) is the correct answer.

15. (A)

$$2^2 \times 5^2 = 4 \times 25$$
$$= 100$$
$$= 10^2$$

Therefore, (A) is the correct answer.

Answers and Solutions
IAAT Practice Test 1 Section 2

Answers

1. C	2. L	3. B	4. J	5. B
6. M	7. C	8. L	9. C	10. L
11. C	12. M	13. A	14. L	15. A

Solutions

1. (C)

   The total number of athletes in Solomon high school is $58 + 52 + 48 + 42 = 200$. Therefore, (C) is the correct answer.

2. (L)

   Arrange the numbers of the data set from least to greatest: $\{42, 48, 52, 58\}$. The median number of athletes participating in a sport is the average of the 2nd and 3rd numbers of the data set. Thus, the median $= \frac{48+52}{2} = 50$. Therefore, (L) is the correct answer.

3. (B)

   The percentage of Solomon high school athletes participated in baseball is $\frac{52}{200} = 0.26 = 26\%$. Therefore, (B) is the correct answer.

4. (J)

   The probability that an athlete chosen at random participates in swimming is $\frac{58}{200} = 0.29$. Therefore, (J) is the correct answer.

5. (B)

   There are 2 vegetables, 4 main dishes, and 2 drinks. Thus, there are $2 \times 4 \times 2 = 16$ different lunches are possible. Therefore, (B) is the correct answer.

6. (M)

   The price of a lunch consisting of 1 carrot, 1 taco, and 1 apple juice is $\$1.25 + \$3.15 + \$1.35 = \$5.75$. Therefore, (M) is the correct answer.

7. (C)

   The cheapest lunch consists of 1 carrot, 1 hot dog, and 1 apple juice. Thus, the price of the cheapest lunch is $\$1.25 + \$2.25 + \$1.35 = \$4.85$. Therefore, (C) is the correct answer.

8. (L)

The most expensive lunch consists of 1 bean, 1 hamburger, and 1 milk. Thus, the price of the most expensive lunch is $1.65 + $3.75 + $1.45 = $6.85. Therefore, (L) is the correct answer.

9. (C)

The total number of the 6th graders in the elementary school is $20 + 30 + 35 + 15 = 100$. Therefore, (C) is the correct answer.

10. (L)

Thirty 6th graders are going to watch romance in a movie theatre, which is twice as many as fifteen 6th graders going to watch comedy. Therefore, (L) is the correct answer.

11. (C)

All multiples of 4 such as $4, 8, 12, \cdots, 24$ are in column 1. So, 25 is in column 2, and 26 in column 3. Therefore, (C) is the correct answer.

12. (M)

The total distance that Mr. Rhee ran is 20 miles. The number of miles that Mr. Rhee ran on Friday is $20 - (3.6 + 4.5 + 3.2 + 4.4) = 4.3$. Therefore, (M) is the correct answer.

13. (A)

	Beginning Time	Ending Time
Period 1	8:30 AM	9:15 AM
Break	9:15 AM	9:25 AM
Period 2	9:25 AM	10:10 AM
Break	10:10 AM	10:20 AM
Period 3	10:20 AM	11:05 AM
Lunch	11:05 AM	12:05 PM

According to the the table above, the first period end at 9:15 AM. Therefore, (A) is the correct answer.

14. (L)

According to the the table shown above, the 3rd period begins at 10:20 AM. Therefore, (L) is the correct answer.

15. (A)

According to the the table shown above, lunch ends at 12:05 PM. Therefore, (A) is the correct answer.

Answers and Solutions

IAAT Practice Test 1 Section 3

Answers

1. D	2. K	3. B	4. J	5. C
6. L	7. D	8. M	9. B	10. M
11. C	12. K	13. C	14. L	15. A

Solutions

1. (D)

   Each number is multiplied by $\frac{1}{3}$ to get the next number. Thus,

   $$81, 27, 9, 3, 1, \frac{1}{3}$$

   Therefore, (D) is the correct answer.

2. (K)

   $$
   \begin{array}{ll}
   2x + 3y = 19 & \text{Substitute 2 for } x \\
   2(2) + 3y = 19 & \text{Subtract 4 from both sides} \\
   3y = 15 & \text{Divide both sides by 3} \\
   y = 5 &
   \end{array}
   $$

   Therefore, (K) is the correct answer.

3. (B)

   The table shows a relationship such that the y-value is 2 more than the x-value, which can be expressed as $y = x + 2$. Therefore, (B) is the correct answer.

4. (J)

   55% of the total number of students T are in blue team. Thus, the number of students in the blue team is $0.55 \times T$ or $0.55T$. Therefore, (J) is the correct answer.

5. (C)

   Joshua is 15 years old now. m years ago, he was $15 - m$ years old. Therefore, (C) is the correct answer.

6. (L)

The area A of a triangle with base b and height h is $A = \frac{1}{2}bh$.

$$A = \frac{1}{2}bh \qquad \text{Substitute 14, for } A \text{ and 14 for } b$$

$$14 = \frac{1}{2}(14)h \qquad \text{Solve for } h$$

$$h = 2$$

Therefore, (L) is the correct answer.

7. (D)

The quotient of x and y is 10 can be expressed as $\frac{x}{y} = 10$. Therefore, (D) is the correct answer.

8. (M)

The table shows a relationship such that output $= 3 \times$ input $- 1$.

$$\text{output} = 3 \times \text{input} - 1 \qquad \text{Substitute 17 for output}$$

$$17 = 3 \times \text{input} - 1 \qquad \text{Add 1 to both sides}$$

$$18 = 3 \times \text{input} \qquad \text{Divide both sides by 3}$$

$$\text{input} = 6$$

Therefore, (M) is the correct answer.

9. (B)

The table in (B) shows a relationship such that the y-value is one more than half the value of x. Therefore, (B) is the correct answer.

10. (M)

The total weight of the luggage in pounds is $2(15) + 3(25) = 30 + 75 = 105$. Therefore, (M) is the correct answer.

11. (C)

Since $-2 < -1 < 3$, $C < A < B$. Therefore, (C) is the correct answer.

12. (K)

x is right of 0 which indicates that x is a positive number. Each tick mark is 0.5. x is in between 0 and first tick mark. So, $0 < x < 0.5$. Since 0.25 satisfies $0 < x < 0.5$, (K) is the correct answer.

13. (C)

The number of pens sold, y, is three less than half the number of pencils sold, x can be expressed as $y = \frac{1}{2}x - 3$. Since the table in (C) satisfies $y = \frac{1}{2}x - 3$, (C) is the correct answer.

14. (L)

Joshua studied two hours a day for five days. Thus, the total number of hours that Joshua studied for the five days is 2×5 or 10 hours. Therefore, (L) is the correct answer.

15. (A)

Jason and other students line up in a row to get lunch. Jason is the 5th from the front and 6th from the back, which means that there are 4 students in front of Jason, and 5 other students behind him. The total number of students in the line is $4 + 1(\text{Jason}) + 5 = 10$. Therefore, (A) is the correct answer.

Answers and Solutions

IAAT Practice Test 1 Section 4

Answers

1. A	2. L	3. A	4. L	5. B
6. L	7. D	8. M	9. A	10. L
11. B	12. J	13. C	14. K	15. C

Solutions

1. (A)

72 is 60 percent of a number, x can be expressed as $72 = 0.6x$. Therefore, (A) is the correct answer.

2. (L)

Note that the inequality symbol is reversed when dividing both sides of the inequality by a negative number. Thus, dividing both sides of the inequality $-2x > 2$ by -2 gives $x < -1$. Therefore, (L) is the correct answer.

3. (A)

$a \clubsuit b = 2a + 3b$. Thus, the value of $3 \clubsuit 2$ is $2(3) + 3(2) = 12$. Therefore, (A) is the correct answer.

4. (L)

$$x = y + 7 \qquad \text{Subtract } y \text{ from both sides}$$
$$x - y = 7$$

Therefore, (L) is the correct answer.

5. (B)

A tulip grows 2 inches in a week. The proportion can be used to find x, the number of weeks needed for the tulip to grow 6 inches is as follows:

$$\frac{2 \text{ inch}}{1 \text{ week}} = \frac{6 \text{ inches}}{x \text{ weeks}}$$

Therefore, (B) is the correct answer.

6. (L)

$$4(x+1) - 3 = 17$$ Add 3 to both sides

$$4(x+1) = 20$$ Divide both sides by 4

$$x + 1 = 5$$ Subtract 1 from both sides

$$x = 4$$

Therefore, (L) is the correct answer.

7. (D)

1 ounce $= c$ cups of coffee   Multiply both sides by 4

4 ounces $= 4c$ cups of coffee

Therefore, (D) is the correct answer.

8. (M)

$2(x+y) = 4$ means that twice the sum of x and y is 4. Therefore, (M) is the correct answer.

9. (A)

$$\frac{3}{2}x + y + \frac{5}{2}x - 2y = \frac{3}{2}x + \frac{5}{2}x + y - 2y$$
$$= \frac{8}{2}x - y$$
$$= 4x - y$$

Therefore, (A) is the correct answer.

10. (L)

$$5x = 6y$$ Substitute 20 for y

$$5x = 120$$ Divide both sides by 5

$$x = 24$$

Therefore, (L) is the correct answer.

11. (B)

$$A = \frac{1}{2}(b_1 + b_2)h$$ Substitute 5 for b_1, 7 for b_2, and 6 for h

$$= \frac{1}{2}(5 + 7)(6)$$

$$= 36$$

Therefore, (B) is the correct answer.

12. (J)

Substitute 2 for x and 8 for y.

$$\sqrt{xy} = \sqrt{2 \times 8} = \sqrt{16} = 4$$

Therefore, (J) is the correct answer.

13. (C)

$$\begin{aligned} -5(x - 2y) &= -5x - (-5)(2y) \\ &= -5x + 10y \\ &= 10y - 5x \end{aligned}$$

Therefore, (C) is the correct answer.

14. (K)

Since the perimeter of a square is $4x$, the length of the square is x. Thus, the area A of the square with side length of x is $A = x^2$. Therefore, (K) is the correct answer.

15. (C)

$S(x)$ is the sum of all the positive integers less than or equal to x. Thus, $S(7) = 1 + 2 + 3 + 4 + 5 + 6 + 7 = 28$. Therefore, (C) is the correct answer.

IAAT PRACTICE TEST 2

SECTION 1
Time — 10 minutes
15 Questions

Directions: Read the information given and choose the best answer for each question. Base your answer only on the information given. The time limit for each section is 10 minutes.

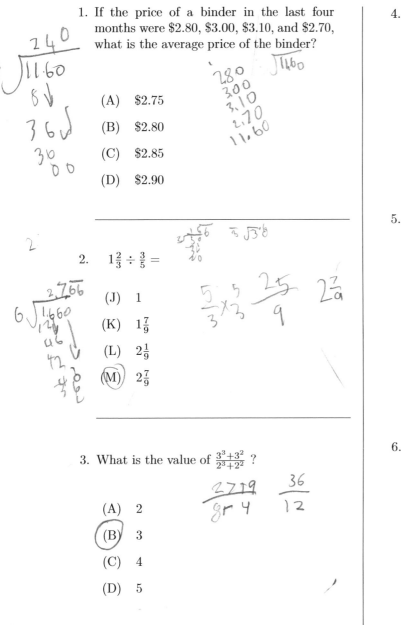

1. If the price of a binder in the last four months were $2.80, $3.00, $3.10, and $2.70, what is the average price of the binder?

   (A) $2.75

   (B) $2.80

   (C) $2.85

   (D) $2.90

2. $1\frac{2}{3} \div \frac{3}{5} =$

   (J) 1

   (K) $1\frac{7}{9}$

   (L) $2\frac{1}{9}$

   (M) $2\frac{7}{9}$

3. What is the value of $\frac{3^3+3^2}{2^3+2^2}$?

   (A) 2

   (B) 3

   (C) 4

   (D) 5

4. Express $20 + 2 + \frac{2}{100}$ in decimal representation.

   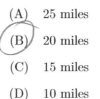

   (J) 22.20

   (K) 22.02

   (L) 20.22

   (M) 20.02

5. If a car travels 60 miles per hour, what is the distance that the car would travel in 20 minutes?

   (A) 25 miles

   (B) 20 miles

   (C) 15 miles

   (D) 10 miles

6. What is the remainder when 107 is divided by 6?

   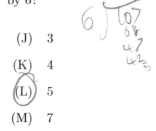

   (J) 3

   (K) 4

   (L) 5

   (M) 7

7. Joshua is 4 feet 6 inches tall. If Jason is $\frac{2}{3}$ of Joshua's height, what is Jason's height in inches? (1 foot = 12 inches)

   (A)   32 inches

   (B)   36 inches

   (C)   40 inches

   (D)   44 inches

---

8. $7.6 + 2.3 \times 3.4 =$

   (J)   33.66

   (K)   27.72

   (L)   18.52

   (M)   15.42

---

9. A clock is malfunctioning. The clock indicates correct time every 12 minutes. For instance, the clock indicates 12pm between 12 pm to 12:11 pm and indicates correct time at 12:12 pm. How many times does the clock indicate correct time between 12:05 pm to 1:05 pm?

   (A)   7 times

   (B)   6 times

   (C)   5 times

   (D)   4 times

---

10. $\frac{1}{3}(1.5 + 0.24) + 4 =$

   (J)   4.58

   (K)   4.38

   (L)   4.18

   (M)   3.98

$$1^2, \ 2^2, \ 3^2, \ 4^2, \ \cdots$$

11. What is the next number in the sequence?

   (A)   36

   (B)   25

   (C)   10

   (D)   5

---

12. Which of the following is NOT true?

   (J) $\frac{3}{4} = 75\%$

   (K) $\frac{3}{5} = 40\%$

   (L) $\frac{1}{5} = 20\%$

   (M) $\frac{1}{8} = 12.5\%$

---

13. If the price of a calculator increases from \$8 to \$10, what is the percent increase?

   (A)   25\%

   (B)   20\%

   (C)   15\%

   (D)   10\%

14. Simplify the expression: $2\frac{3}{5} - 1\frac{3}{4}$

(J) $\frac{17}{20}$

(K) $\frac{4}{5}$

(L) $\frac{3}{4}$

(M) $\frac{7}{10}$

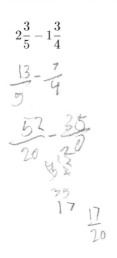

15. Ten students and two chaperons went on a field trip. The total cost of the trip was $240, which was to be equally shared among students. What was amount of money that each student paid for the trip?

(A) $24

(B) $22

(C) $20

(D) $18

STOP

IAAT PRACTICE TEST 2

SECTION 2
Time — 10 minutes
15 Questions

Directions: Read the information given and choose the best answer for each question. Base your answer only on the information given. The time limit for each section is 10 minutes.

Directions: The table below shows the original recipe for 8 crepes. Use the table to answer questions 1 – 4.

Ingredients	Amount
All-purpose flour	1 cup
Milk	$\frac{1}{2}$ cup
Water	$\frac{1}{2}$ cup
Eggs	2
Butter	2 table spoons

1. Sue wants to make 16 crepes. How much of all-purpose flour does she need according to the recipe?

   (A)   5 cups

   (B)   4 cups

   (C)   3 cups

   (D)   2 cups

2. If Sue uses $\frac{1}{2}$ cup of all-purpose flour to make crepes, how much milk does the recipe call for?

   (J) $\frac{1}{2}$ cup

   (K) $\frac{1}{3}$ cup

   (L) $\frac{1}{4}$ cup

   (M) $\frac{1}{5}$ cup

3. One butter stick is equivalent to 8 table spoons. If Sue has one butter stick, how many crepes is she able to make?

   (A)   16 crepes

   (B)   24 crepes

   (C)   32 crepes

   (D)   40 crepes

4. If She uses $\frac{3}{2}$ cups of water to make crepes, how many eggs does the recipe call for?

   (J)   6 eggs

   (K)   8 eggs

   (L)   10 eggs

   (M)   12 eggs

Directions: 300 people surveyed about their favorite food. The graph shows the result in decimal. Use the graph to answer questions 5 − 8.

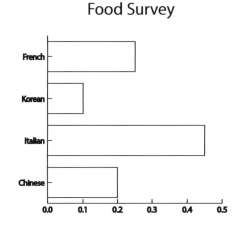

Food Survey

5. According to the graph above, which food is the most liked food among the people who surveyed?

  (A) French

  (B) Korean

  (C) Italian

  (D) Chinese

6. What percentage of the people who surveyed chose Korean food as their favorite?

  (J) 25%

  (K) 20%

  (L) 15%

  (M) 10%

7. Among the people who surveyed, which of the following best represents the number of people who chose Italian as their favorite food?

  (A) 150

  (B) 135

  (C) 120

  (D) 105

8. How many more people chose Italian as their favorite food than people who chose French as their favorite food?

  (J) 100

  (K) 80

  (L) 60

  (M) 40

Item	Cost
Bread	$2.50
Cheese	$2.75
Butter	$2.25
Ham	$4.50

9. Mr. Rhee went to the store to purchase the following items shown above last week. If Mr. Rhee pays 25% more on the same items that he purchased last week, how much would he pay?

(A) $16

(B) $15

(C) $14

(D) $13

10. Jason earned $10 in January, $15 in February, and $20 in March. If he earns more as the pattern continues, what is the amount that Jason expects to earn in August?

(J) $60

(K) $55

(L) $50

(M) $45

$\{11, 9, 7, 15, 13\}$

11. What is the difference of the mean and the median of the data set shown above?

(A) 0

(B) 1

(C) 2

(D) 4

Directions: The table below shows the number of miles that Joshua and Jason ran from Monday to Thursday. Use the table to answer questions 12 − 15.

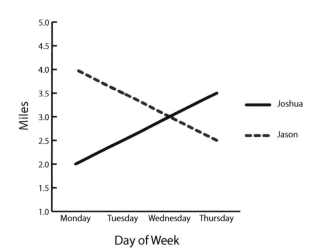

12. How many miles did Joshua run on Monday?

(J) 2 miles

(K) 2.5 miles

(L) 3 miles

(M) 4 miles

13. Which of the day did Jason run least?

    (A)   Monday

    (B)   Tuesday

    (C)   Wednesday

    (D)   Thursday

14. Which day did Joshua and Jason run the same number of miles?

    (J)   Monday

    (K)   Tuesday

    (L)   Wednesday

    (M)   Thursday

15. How many more miles did Joshua run than Jason on Thursday?

    (A)   1 miles

    (B)   2 miles

    (C)   3 miles

    (D)   4 miles

IAAT PRACTICE TEST 2

SECTION 3
Time — 10 minutes
15 Questions

Directions: Read the information given and choose the best answer for each question. Base your answer only on the information given. The time limit for each section is 10 minutes.

1. The sound travels at about 343.2 meters per second. Which of the following best approximates the distance that the sound travels in 5 seconds?

    (A)   1500 meters

    (B)   1600 meters

    (C)   1700 meters

    (D)   1800 meters

2. Which of the following equation best represents the following verbal phrase? The number of red marbles, y, is 25% more than the number of blue marbles, x.

    (J) $y = 1.25x$

    (K) $y = x$

    (L) $y = 0.75x$

    (M) $y = 0.25x$

3. What is the value of y for the equation $y = \frac{k}{x}$ if $k = -12$ and $x = -3$?

    (A)   4

    (B) $\frac{1}{4}$

    (C) $-\frac{1}{4}$

    (D) -4

4. Which of the following table represents a function?

    (J)
x	0	0	0	0
y	-1	0	1	2

    (K)
x	1	1	2	3
y	2	3	4	5

    (L)
x	1	2	2	3
y	-1	-3	-2	-3

    (M)
x	1	2	3	4
y	1	1	1	1

5. The number of pens is three more than twice the number of notebooks. If the number of the notebooks is 7, what is the number of pens?

    (A)   18

    (B)   17

    (C)   15

    (D)   14

6. The ratio of x to y is $\frac{1}{2}$. Which of the following tables represent this relationship?

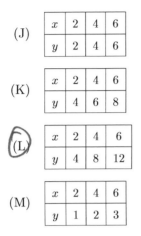

(J)

x	2	4	6
y	2	4	6

(K)

x	2	4	6
y	4	6	8

(L)

x	2	4	6
y	4	8	12

(M)

x	2	4	6
y	1	2	3

Input	Output
3	8
4	9
7	12
	17

7. Observe the numbers in the two columns in order to determine which of the following value should be in the empty cell.

(A) 11

(B) 12

(C) 13

(D) 14

$$-2(3-4)$$

8. Which of the following expression is equivalent to the expression shown above?

(J) $3 \times -2 + 4 \times 2$

(K) $3 \times -2 - 4 \times 2$

(L) $3 \times 2 + 4 \times 2$

(M) $3 \times 2 - 4 \times 2$

9. If $0.2x = y$, what is the value of x if $y = 5$?

(A) 30

(B) 25

(C) 20

(D) 15

x	y
1	1
3	27
5	125
6	216

10. The table shows four pairs of x and y values. Which is true for all values in the table shown above?

(J) $y = x^3$

(K) $y = x^2$

(L) $y = 2x$

(M) $y = x + 2$

11. Which of the following ordered pairs does the line $y = \frac{1}{3}x$ passes through?

   (A) $(0,0)$ and $(3,1)$

   (B) $(1,0)$ and $(2,0)$

   (C) $(3,1)$ and $(6,3)$

   (D) $(5,2)$ and $(9,6)$

12. The Euler's formula says that the sum of the number of faces, F, and the number of vertices, V, equals the number of edges, E, plus 2. Which of the following expression best represents the Euler's formula?

   (J) $F + V = E + 2$

   (K) $F - V = E + 2$

   (L) $F + V = E - 2$

   (M) $F - V = E - 2$

13. Which of the following table best represents the following verbal relationship? The number of DVD sold, y, is 50% of the number of TV sold, x.

   (A)

x	100	200	300	400
y	50	100	150	200

   (B)

x	100	200	300	400
y	150	300	450	600

   (C)

x	100	200	300	400
y	200	400	600	800

   (D)

x	100	200	300	400
y	300	500	700	900

x	y
5	9
6	11
7	13
8	

14. Observe the numbers in the two columns in order to determine which of the following value should be in the empty cell.

   (J)   17

   (K)   16

   (L)   15

   (M)   14

15. Which of the following equations best represent the following verbal relationship? The quotient of x and y is 5 less z.

   (A) $\frac{x}{y} = 5 - z$

   (B) $\frac{y}{x} = 5 - z$

   (C) $\frac{x}{y} = z - 5$

   (D) $\frac{y}{x} = z - 5$

STOP

IAAT PRACTICE TEST 2

SECTION 4
Time — 10 minutes
15 Questions

Directions: Read the information given and choose the best answer for each question. Base your answer only on the information given. The time limit for each section is 10 minutes.

1. A box contains x number of cookies. If Joshua, Jason, and Sue are going to share the same number of cookies, which of the following expression represents the number of cookies that Jason will have?

   (A) $x + 3$

   (B) $3x$

   (C) $\frac{x}{3}$

   (D) $\frac{3}{x}$

2. Which of the following value of x satisfies the inequality $4 - x < 2$?

   (J) 3

   (K) 2

   (L) 1

   (M) 0

3. Which of the following equation is NOT true?

   (A) $\frac{2}{6} = \frac{1}{3}$

   (B) $\frac{0}{2} = 0$

   (C) $\frac{1}{0} = $ Undefined

   (D) $\frac{0}{0} = 1$

4. Simplify the expression: $2x + 2x + 2x$

   (J) $8x^3$

   (K) $6x^3$

   (L) $8x$

   (M) $6x$

5. Solve for x: $\frac{1}{2}x + 1 = 3$

   (A) 8

   (B) 6

   (C) 4

   (D) 2

6. If $2x + 2y = 6$, what is the value of $3x + 3y$?

   (J) 7

   (K) 8

   (L) 9

   (M) 10

7. The price of a pair of shoes is $\$n$. If sales tax rate is 8%, which of the following expression represents the total amount after the tax?

 (A) $8n$

 (B) $1.8n$

 (C) $1.08n$

 (D) $0.8n$

---

six less a number, y.

8. How is the following verbal phrase above expressed algebraically?

 (J) $6y$

 (K) $\frac{6}{y}$

 (L) $y - 6$

 (M) $6 - y$

---

9. If $\frac{x}{3} = z$, which of the following expression represents $3z$?

 (A) x

 (B) $\frac{1}{x}$

 (C) 3

 (D) $\frac{1}{3}$

---

10. Solve for x: $y + 2x = y + 10$

 (J) 5

 (K) 4

 (L) 3

 (M) 2

Twice the sum of 4 and x is 12.

11. Solve for x of the following verbal phrase above.

 (A) 5

 (B) 4

 (C) 3

 (D) 2

---

12. Solve the inequality: $-\frac{1}{3}x + 2 > -1$

 (J) $x > -9$

 (K) $x < -9$

 (L) $x > 9$

 (M) $x < 9$

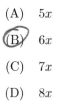

---

13. Two identical squares with side length x are put together to form a rectangle. Which of the following best represents the perimeter of the rectangle?

 (A) $5x$

 (B) $6x$

 (C) $7x$

 (D) $8x$

14. If Joshua reads p pages of a book every day, at this rate, how many pages would Joshua read in two weeks?

   (J) $14p$

   (K) $2p$

   (L) $\frac{p}{2}$

   (M) $\frac{p}{14}$

15. Jason had \$600 in his savings account. If he wishes to have a total of \$2100 in six weeks, how much money does he need to save in each week?

   (A)   \$350

   (B)   \$300

   (C)   \$250

   (D)   \$200

STOP

Answers and Solutions

IAAT Practice Test 2 Section 1

Answers

1. D	2. M	3. B	4. K	5. B
6. L	7. B	8. M	9. C	10. J
11. B	12. K	13. A	14. J	15. A

Solutions

1. (D)

   The average price of the binder is $\dfrac{2.8 + 3 + 3.1 + 2.7}{4} = \dfrac{11.6}{4} = 2.9$. Therefore, (D) is the correct answer.

2. (M)

$$1\frac{2}{3} \div \frac{3}{5} = \frac{5}{3} \times \frac{5}{3} = \frac{25}{9} = 2\frac{7}{9}$$

   Therefore, (M) is the correct answer.

3. (B)

$$\frac{3^3 + 3^2}{2^3 + 2^2} = \frac{27 + 9}{8 + 4} = \frac{36}{12} = 3.$$

   Therefore, (B) is the correct answer.

4. (K)

   $\frac{2}{100} = 0.02$. Thus, $20 + 2 + \frac{2}{100} = 22.02$. Therefore, (K) is the correct answer.

5. (B)

   20 minutes is $\frac{20 \text{ minutes}}{60 \text{ minutes}} = \frac{1}{3}$ hour.

   $$\text{In } 1 \text{ hour} = 60 \text{ miles} \qquad\qquad \text{Multiply both sides by } \frac{1}{3}$$

   $$\text{In } \frac{1}{3} \text{ hour} = 20 \text{ miles}$$

   Therefore, (B) is the correct answer.

6. (L)

when 107 is divided by 6, the quotient is 17 and the remainder is 5. Therefore, (L) is the correct answer.

7. (B)

1 foot $= 12$ inches. Joshua is 4 feet 6 inches tall, which is equal to $4 \times 12 + 6 = 54$ inches. Since Jason is $\frac{2}{3}$ of Joshua's height, he is $\frac{2}{3} \times 54 = 36$ inches. Therefore, (B) is the correct answer.

8. (M)

$$7.6 + 2.3 \times 3.4 = 7.6 + 7.82 = 15.42$$

Therefore, (M) is the correct answer.

9. (C)

Between 12:05 pm to 1:05 pm, the clock indicates correct time five times: at 12:12 pm, 12:24 pm, 12:36 pm, 12:48 pm, and 1:00 pm. Therefore, (C) is the correct answer.

10. (J)

$$\frac{1}{3}(1.5 + 0.24) + 4 = \frac{1}{3}(1.74) + 4 = 0.58 + 4 = 4.58$$

Therefore, (J) is the correct answer.

11. (B)

The next number in the sequence is $5^2 = 25$. Therefore, (B) is the correct answer.

12. (K)

$\frac{3}{5} = 0.6 = 60\%$. Therefore, (K) is the correct answer.

13. (A)

$$\begin{aligned}
\text{The percent increase} &= \frac{\text{Final} - \text{Initial}}{\text{Initial}} \times 100\% \\
&= \frac{10 - 8}{8} \times 100\% \\
&= 25\%
\end{aligned}$$

Therefore, (A) is the correct answer.

14. (J)

$$2\frac{3}{5} - 1\frac{3}{4} = \frac{13}{5} - \frac{7}{4} = \frac{52}{20} - \frac{35}{20} = \frac{17}{20}$$

Therefore, (J) is the correct answer.

15. (A)

The total cost of the trip was $240, which was to be equally shared among ten students. Thus, the amount of money that each student paid for the trip was $\frac{240}{10} = 24$. Therefore, (A) is the correct answer.

Answers and Solutions

IAAT Practice Test 2 Section 2

Answers

1. D	2. L	3. C	4. J	5. C
6. M	7. B	8. L	9. B	10. M
11. A	12. J	13. D	14. L	15. A

Solutions

1. (D)

Since Sue wants to make 16 crepes, she needs double the amount of ingredients shown on the table.

$$8 \text{ crepes} = 1 \text{ cup of flour} \qquad \text{Multiply both sides by 2}$$
$$16 \text{ crepes} = 2 \text{ cups of flour}$$

Therefore, (D) is the correct answer.

2. (L)

$$1 \text{ cup of flour} = \frac{1}{2} \text{ cup of milk} \qquad \text{Multiply both sides by } \frac{1}{2}$$
$$\frac{1}{2} \text{ cup of flour} = \frac{1}{4} \text{ cup of milk}$$

Therefore, (L) is the correct answer.

3. (C)

$$2 \text{ table spoons of butter} = 8 \text{ crepes} \qquad \text{Multiply both sides by 4}$$
$$8 \text{ table spoons of butter} = 32 \text{ crepes}$$

Therefore, (C) is the correct answer.

4. (J)

$$\frac{1}{2} \text{ cup of water} = 8 \text{ crepes} = 2 \text{ eggs} \qquad \text{Multiply all sides by 3}$$
$$\frac{3}{2} \text{ cup of water} = 24 \text{ crepes} = 6 \text{ eggs}$$

Therefore, (J) is the correct answer.

5. (C)

According to the graph above, which food is the most liked food among the people who surveyed is Italian. Therefore, (C) is the correct answer.

6. (M)

The percentage of the people who surveyed chose Korean food as their favorite is 0.1 or 10%. Therefore, (M) is the correct answer.

7. (B)

45% of people who surveyed chose Italian food as their favorite. Thus, the number of people who chose Italian is $0.45 \times 300 = 135$. Therefore, (B) is the correct answer.

8. (L)

The number of people who chose Italian is 135. 25% of people who surveyed chose French food as their favorite. So, the number of people who chose French is $0.25 \times 300 = 75$. Thus, $135 - 75$ or 60 more people chose Italian than people who chose French. Therefore, (L) is the correct answer.

9. (B)

The total cost for item that Mr. purchased was $\$2.5 + \$2.75 + \$2.25 + \$4.5 = \$12$. Since Mr. Rhee pays 25% more on the same items that he purchased, he would pay $\$12 + 0.25(\$12)$ or $1.25 \times \$12 = \$15$. Therefore, (B) is the correct answer.

10. (M)

Jan	Feb	Mar	Apr	May	Jun	Jul	Aug
$10	$15	$20	$25	$30	$35	$40	$45

Therefore, (M) is the correct answer.

11. (A)

The mean is $\dfrac{11 + 9 + 7 + 15 + 13}{5} = \dfrac{55}{5} = 11$. Arrange the numbers from least to greatest: $\{7, 9, 11, 13, 15\}$. The median is the middle number, which is 11. Thus, the difference of the mean and the median of the data set is $11 - 11 = 0$. Therefore, (A) is the correct answer.

12. (J)

The number of miles that Joshua ran on Monday is 2 miles. Therefore, (J) is the correct answer.

13. (D)

Jason ran least on Thursday. Therefore, (D) is the correct answer.

14. (L)

On Wednesday, both Joshua and Jason ran 3 miles. Therefore, (L) is the correct answer.

15. (A)

On Thursday, Joshua ran 3.5 miles, and Jason ran 2.5 miles. Thus, Joshua ran 1 mile more than Jason did on Thursday. Therefore, (A) is the correct answer.

Answers and Solutions

IAAT Practice Test 2 Section 3

Answers

1. C	2. J	3. A	4. M	5. B
6. L	7. B	8. J	9. B	10. J
11. A	12. J	13. A	14. L	15. A

Solutions

1. (C)

    $343.2 \times 5 = 1716 \approx 1700$. Therefore, (C) is the correct answer.

2. (J)

    25% of x is $0.25x$. Since y is 25% more than x, it can be expressed as $y = x + 0.25x = 1.25x$. Therefore, (J) is the correct answer.

3. (A)

    $k = -12$ and $x = -3$. Thus, $y = \dfrac{k}{x} = \dfrac{-12}{-3} = 4$. Therefore, (A) is the correct answer.

4. (M)

    A function is a set of ordered pairs whose x-values are **NOT** repeated. Since x-values in table (M) are not repeated, (M) is the correct answer.

5. (B)

    Let x be the number of notebooks and y be the the number of pens. The number of pens is three more than twice the number of notebooks can be expressed as $y = 2x + 3$. When $x = 7$, $y = 2x + 3 = 2(7) + 3 = 17$. Thus, the number of pens is 17. Therefore, (B) is the correct answer.

6. (L)

    The ratio of x to y is $\frac{1}{2}$ means that y-values are twice x-values. The table in (L) contains a set of ordered pairs $\{(2, 4), (4, 8), (6, 12)\}$ that show the relationship. Therefore, (L) is the correct answer.

7. (B)

    The table shows a relationship such that Output = Input + 5. Thus, when Input = 12, Output = 17. Therefore, (B) is the correct answer.

8. (J)

$$-2(3-4) = -2 \times 3 - (-2) \times 4$$
$$= 3 \times -2 + 2 \times 4$$
$$= 3 \times -2 + 4 \times 2$$

Therefore, (J) is the correct answer.

9. (B)

Since $0.2 = \frac{1}{5}$, $0.2x = y$ can be written as $\frac{1}{5}x = y$.

$$\frac{1}{5}x = y \qquad\qquad \text{Substitute 5 for } y$$
$$\frac{1}{5}x = 5 \qquad\qquad \text{Multiply both sides by 5}$$
$$x = 25$$

Therefore, (B) is the correct answer.

10. (J)

Since $1 = 1^3$, $27 = 3^3$, and $125 = 5^3$, $y = x^3$. Therefore, (J) is the correct answer.

11. (A)

Substituting $x = 0$ into $y = \frac{1}{3}x$ gives $y = 0$. Additionally, substituting $x = 3$ into $y = \frac{1}{3}x$ gives $y = 1$. It means that two ordered pairs $(0, 0)$ and $(3, 1)$ are on the line $y = \frac{1}{3}x$. Therefore, (A) is the correct answer.

12. (J)

The sum of the number of faces, F, and the number of vertices, V, equals the number of edges, E, plus 2 can be expressed as $F + V = E + 2$. Therefore, (J) is the correct answer.

13. (A)

$50\% = 0.5 = \frac{1}{2}$. The number of DVD sold, y, is 50% of the number of TV sold, x can be expressed as $y = \frac{1}{2}x$. Since the table in (A) satisfies $y = \frac{1}{2}x$, (A) is the correct answer.

14. (L)

The y-value is one less than twice the x-value, which can be expressed as $y = 2x - 1$. Thus, when $x = 8$, $y = 2(8) - 1 = 15$. Therefore, (L) is the correct answer.

15. (A)

The quotient of x and y can be expressed as $\frac{x}{y}$, and 5 less z can be expressed as $5 - z$. Thus, the quotient of x and y is 5 less z can be expressed as $\frac{x}{y} = 5 - z$. Therefore, (A) is the correct answer.

Answers and Solutions
IAAT Practice Test 2 Section 4

Answers

1. C	2. J	3. D	4. M	5. C
6. L	7. C	8. M	9. A	10. J
11. D	12. M	13. B	14. J	15. C

Solutions

1. (C)

   Joshua, Jason, and Sue share x number of cookies. Thus, the number of cookies that Jason will have is $\dfrac{x}{3}$. Therefore, (C) is the correct answer.

2. (J)

   Substituting 3 for x in $4 - x < 2$ satisfies the inequality $4 - 3 < 2$ or $1 < 2$. Therefore, (J) is the correct answer.

3. (D)

   Since $\frac{0}{0}$ = undefined, (D) is the correct answer.

4. (M)

   $2x + 2x + 2x = 6x$. Therefore, (M) is the correct answer.

5. (C)

$$\frac{1}{2}x + 1 = 3 \qquad \text{Subtract 1 from both sides}$$
$$\frac{1}{2}x = 2 \qquad \text{Multiply both sides by 2}$$
$$x = 4$$

   Therefore, (C) is the correct answer.

6. (L)

$$2x + 2y = 6 \qquad \text{Divide both sides by 2}$$
$$x + y = 3 \qquad \text{Multiply both sides by 3}$$
$$3x + 3y = 9$$

   Therefore, (L) is the correct answer.

7. (C)

$8\% = 0.08$. The tax amount is $0.08 \times n$ or $0.08n$. Thus, the total amount after the tax is $n + 0.08n$ or $1.08n$. Therefore, (C) is the correct answer.

8. (M)

six less a number, y can be expressed as $6 - y$. Therefore, (M) is the correct answer.

9. (A)

$$\frac{x}{3} = z \qquad \text{Multiply both sides by 3}$$
$$x = 3z$$

Therefore, (A) is the correct answer.

10. (J)

$$y + 2x = y + 10 \qquad \text{Subtract } y \text{ from both sides}$$
$$2x = 10 \qquad \text{Divide both sides by 2}$$
$$x = 5$$

Therefore, (J) is the correct answer.

11. (D)

Twice the sum of 4 and x is 12 can be written as $2(x + 4) = 12$.

$$2(x + 4) = 12 \qquad \text{Divide both sides by 2}$$
$$x + 4 = 6 \qquad \text{Subtract 4 from both sides}$$
$$x = 2$$

Therefore, (D) is the correct answer.

12. (M)

$$-\frac{1}{3}x + 2 > -1 \qquad \text{Subtract 2 from both sides}$$
$$-\frac{1}{3}x > -3 \qquad \text{Multiply both sides by } -3$$
$$x < 9 \qquad \text{Reverse the inequality symbol}$$

Therefore, (M) is the correct answer.

13. (B)

Two identical squares with side length x are put together to form a rectangle as shown below.

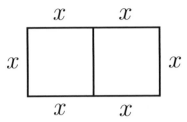

The perimeter of the rectangle is the distance around the rectangle. Thus, the perimeter of the rectangle is $x + x + x + x + x + x = 6x$. Therefore, (B) is the correct answer.

14. (J)

There are 14 days in 2 weeks. Since Joshua reads p pages every day, the number of pages that Joshua would read in 14 days is $14 \times p$ or $14p$. Therefore, (J) is the correct answer.

15. (C)

Jason had \$600 in his savings account. He needs to save \$1500 in 6 weeks to have a total of \$2100. Thus, the amount of money that he need to save in each week is $\frac{\$1500}{6} = \$250$. Therefore, (C) is the correct answer.

IAAT PRACTICE TEST 3

SECTION 1
Time — 10 minutes
15 Questions

Directions: Read the information given and choose the best answer for each question. Base your answer only on the information given. The time limit for each section is 10 minutes.

1. Evaluate: 0.31×0.4

   (A) 0.0124

   (B) 0.124

   (C) 1.24

   (D) 12.4

$$1, \ 5, \ 9, \ 13, \cdots$$

2. Joshua starts with the number 1 and counts by 4s. This results in the sequence as shown above. What is the 6th number in the sequence?

   (J) 19

   (K) 20

   (L) 21

   (M) 22

3. Evaluate: $(2 \times 4 \times 6 \times 8) \div (1 \times 2 \times 3 \times 4)$

   (A) 12

   (B) 14

   (C) 15

   (D) 16

4. Jason has a map that uses a scale of 1 inch for every 9 miles. If Jason drives 234 miles from home to his friend's house, which of the following number best represents, in inches, the distance that he drives on the map?

   (J) 26

   (K) 27

   (L) 28

   (M) 29

5. Evaluate: $2\frac{1}{4} - \frac{5}{8}$

   (A) $1\frac{5}{8}$

   (B) $1\frac{1}{2}$

   (C) $1\frac{3}{8}$

   (D) $1\frac{1}{4}$

6. Mr. Rhee can make 1 pancake in 12 minutes. How many total pancakes can he make in 2 hours?

   (J) 12

   (K) 10

   (L) 8

   (M) 5

7. A bank loaned $500 to a business man. The business man paid the amount borrowed plus 20% interest. What was the total amount of money that the business man paid to the bank?

(A) $550

(B) $600

(C) $650

(D) $700

8. What is the least common multiple (LCM) of 2, 3, and 4 ?

(J) 24

(K) 18

(L) 16

(M) 12

9. Which set is ordered from greatest to least?

(A) $\{0.15, \frac{1}{8}, \frac{1}{5}, 25\%\}$

(B) $\{25\%, \frac{1}{5}, 0.15, \frac{1}{8}\}$

(C) $\{\frac{1}{8}, 0.15, \frac{1}{5}, 25\%\}$

(D) $\{25\%, 0.15, \frac{1}{5}, \frac{1}{8}\}$

10. There are 200 students in a school. If there are 56 students taking Spanish, what percent of the student in the school taking Spanish?

(J) 28%

(K) 36%

(L) 45%

(M) 56%

11. Joshua ate $\frac{2}{3}$ of a pizza. After one hour, he ate $\frac{1}{3}$ of the remaining pizza. What fractional part of the pizza did Joshua eat?

(A) $\frac{5}{9}$

(B) $\frac{2}{3}$

(C) $\frac{7}{9}$

(D) $\frac{8}{9}$

$$23 + 45 + \square + 69 = 200$$

12. What number goes to the box shown above so that the equation is true?

(J) 43

(K) 53

(L) 63

(M) 73

13. Mr. Rhee ran 1 hour and 14 minutes. How many minutes did he run?

(A) 64 minutes

(B) 74 minutes

(C) 94 minutes

(D) 114 minutes

14. Joshua is 7 years older than Jason. Sue is 23 years older than Jason. How much older than Joshua is Sue?

(J)   11

(K)   16

(L)   25

(M)   30

15. Jason notices that he is the 12th person from the front of the line and is 11th person from the back of the line. How many people are in the line?

(A)   21

(B)   22

(C)   23

(D)   24

14/15

STOP

IAAT PRACTICE TEST 3

SECTION 2
Time — 10 minutes
15 Questions

Directions: Read the information given and choose the best answer for each question. Base your answer only on the information given. The time limit for each section is 10 minutes.

Directions: The bar graph below shows the number of hours of sleep, study, and play for Jason, Sue, and Joshua. Use the graph to answer questions 1−4.

Daily Schedule

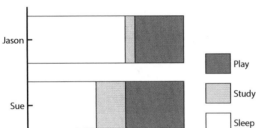

1. Who slept the most?

   (A) Jason

   (B) Sue

   (C) Joshua

   (D) Cannot be determined

2. Who played the least?

   (J) Jason

   (K) Sue

   (L) Joshua

   (M) Cannot be determined

3. Which of the following best represents the number of hours that Sue studied?

   (A) 1

   (B) 3

   (C) 5

   (D) 7

4. How many more hours did Sue play than Joshua?

   (J) 2

   (K) 4

   (L) 6

   (M) 8

Directions: Use the following graph to answer questions 5 – 8.

The Price of Gasoline over 5 Months

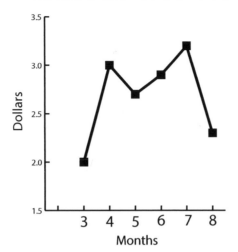

5. Which period did the price of gasoline decrease most?

(A) From July to August

(B) From June to July

(C) From May to June

(D) From April to May

6. Which of the following price best represents the price of gasoline in May?

(J) $2.2

(K) $2.4

(L) $2.5

(M) $2.7

7. What is the percent increase of the price of gasoline from March to April?

(A) 200%

(B) 100%

(C) 75%

(D) 50%

8. How much higher than the price of gasoline in June is the price of the gasoline in July?

(J) $0.1

(K) $0.25

(L) $0.5

(M) $1

Favorite Color	Students
Red	9
Blue	17
Green	8
White	13
Other	3

9. Fifty students were asked to name their one favorite color. The chart above shows the results. What percent of students named blue?

(A) 34%

(B) 17%

(C) 12%

(D) 8.5%

10. Joshua, Jason, and 13 other students line up in a row to get lunch. Joshua is the 7th from the front and Jason is 3rd from the back. How many students are there between Joshua and Jason? (Do not count Joshua and Jason.)

(J) 4

(K) 5

(L) 6

(M) 7

M	T	W	R	F
22	52		17	33

11. The table above shows the amount of books sold in 5 days. If the total number of books sold is 189, which of the following value belongs in the empty cell?

(A) 60

(B) 65

(C) 68

(D) 75

12. Four soccer teams A, B, C, and D compete against each other in a tournament. Each team plays against every other team only once. How many games are played in all?

(J) 8

(K) 7

(L) 6

(M) 5

13. 2 pears and 2 apples collectively weigh 24 ounces. 3 pears and 2 apples collectively weigh 29 ounces. Assuming that all the pears and apples respectively weigh the same, how much does a pear weigh?

(A) 2

(B) 3

(C) 4

(D) 5

Extra-Curricular	Percent
Outdoor Activities	26
Music	21
Chess	7
Reading	18
Playing Games	13
Others	15

14. Jason surveyed students at his school and asked each to select one favorite extra-curricular activity. The percents of the total number of students who responded for each activity are displayed in the table above. If 54 students selected reading as their favorite extra-curricular activity, how many total number of students responded to Jason's survey?

(J) 200

(K) 225

(L) 250

(M) 300

15. Mr. Rhee runs 90 miles in two weeks. What is the average number of miles Mr. Rhee run per day if he runs 5 days a week?

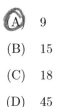 (A) 9

(B) 15

(C) 18

(D) 45

STOP

IAAT PRACTICE TEST 3

SECTION 3
Time — 10 minutes
15 Questions

Directions: Read the information given and choose the best answer for each question. Base your answer only on the information given. The time limit for each section is 10 minutes.

1. A car travels at 60 miles per hour. Which of the following best represents the distance that the car travels in 30 minutes?

   (A)   50 miles

   (B)   40 miles

   (C)   30 miles

   (D)   20 miles

2. If $y = kx$ and $k = -3$, what is the value of y when $x = -2$?

   (J)   6

   (K) $\dfrac{1}{6}$

   (L) $-\dfrac{1}{6}$

   (M) -6

3. If a recipe for 6 pancakes calls for 6 eggs and 3 cups of flour, how many eggs and cups of flour are need to make 4 pancakes?

   (A)   3 eggs and 1.5 cups of flour

   (B)   3 eggs and 2 cups of flour

   (C)   4 eggs and 1.5 cups of flour

   (D)   4 eggs and 2 cups of flour

4. In a right triangle, the hypotenuse, side opposite the right angle, is c and other two sides are a and b. The Pythagorean theorem states that the square of the hypotenuse is equal to the sum of the squares of the other two sides. Which of the following equations best represent the Pythagorean theorem?

   (J) $c^2 = a^2 + b^2$

   (K) $c^2 = (a + b)^2$

   (L) $c^2 = a + b$

   (M) $2c = 2(a + b)$

5. The perimeter of a rectangle is 30. If the length of the rectangle is 10, then what is the area of the rectangle?

   (A)   45

   (B)   50

   (C)   55

   (D)   60

6. If $2x = 3y$, which of the following tables represent this relationship?

(J)
x	3	6	9
y	4	7	10

(K)
x	3	6	9
y	6	12	18

(L)
x	3	6	9
y	2	4	6

(M)
x	3	6	9
y	4	8	12

7. At sea level, the pressure is 10 pounds per square inches. If the pressure increases 15 pounds for every 10 meters of water depth, what is the pressure at the depth of 50 meters below the sea level?

(A) 65

(B) 75

(C) 85

(D) 95

8. The volume V of a cylinder is $V = \pi r^2 h$, where r is the radius and h is the height. If the radius of the cylinder is 3 and the volume of the cylinder is 27π, what is the height of the cylinder?

(J) 6

(K) 5

(L) 4

(M) 3

9. Below shows a function of x containing four ordered pairs (x, y).

$$\{(2, 2), (3, 6), (5, 7), (6, 9)\}$$

What is the range of the function?

(A) $\{2, 6, 7, 9\}$

(B) $\{2, 4, 6, 8\}$

(C) $\{2, 3, 5, 7\}$

(D) $\{1, 3, 5, 7\}$

x	10	20	30	40
y	200	400	600	800

10. The table shows four pairs of x and y values. Which is true for all values in the table shown above?

(J) $y = x + 190$

(K) $y = 20x$

(L) $y = 2x^2$

(M) $y = 2(x + 10)$

x	-2	0	1
y	0	2	3

11. Which graph best represents the line defined by the table of ordered pairs?

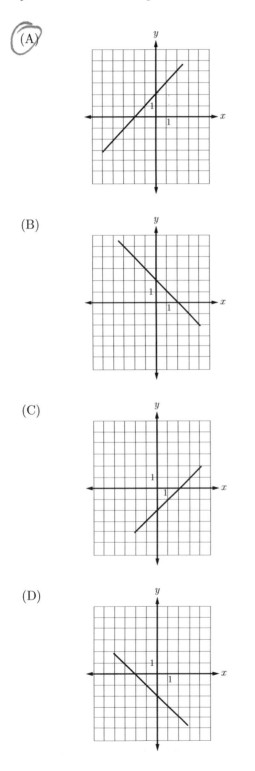

(A)

(B)

(C)

(D)

12. If x increases by 1, y decreases by 2, which of the following equations best represent this relationship?

(J)　$y = 2x + 1$

(K)　$y = x + 2$

(L)　$y = -x - 2$

(M)　$y = -2x - 1$

13. Which table could be used to graph $y = \dfrac{1}{2}x - 3$?

(A)

x	2	4	6	8
y	1	2	3	4

(B)

x	2	4	6	8
y	-2	-1	0	1

(C)

x	2	4	6	8
y	-1	0	1	2

(D)

x	2	4	6	8
y	0	1	2	3

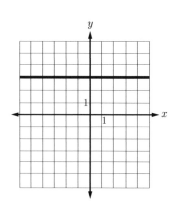

14. Which could be table of ordered pairs that was used to graph the function of x shown above ?

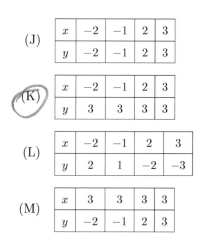

(J)

x	-2	-1	2	3
y	-2	-1	2	3

(K)

x	-2	-1	2	3
y	3	3	3	3

(L)

x	-2	-1	2	3
y	2	1	-2	-3

(M)

x	3	3	3	3
y	-2	-1	2	3

15. A trapezoid has two bases, b_1 and b_2, and height h. In order to find the area A of the Trapezoid, take the sum of its bases, multiply the sum by the height of the trapezoid, and then divide the result by 2. Which of the following formulas best represent the area of the trapezoid?

(A) $A = 2h(b_1 + b_2)$

(B) $A = 2hb_1 + b_2$

(C) $A = \frac{1}{2}b_1h + b_2$

(D) $A = \frac{1}{2}(b_1 + b_2)h$

STOP

IAAT PRACTICE TEST 3

SECTION 4
Time — 10 minutes
15 Questions

Directions: Read the information given and choose the best answer for each question. Base your answer only on the information given. The time limit for each section is 10 minutes.

1. Joshua is x years old now. How old was he 10 years ago in terms of x ?

  (A) $10x$

  (B) $10 - x$

  (C) $x + 10$

  (D) $x - 10$

2. Which of the following equation is NOT equivalent to $x - 3 = 2$?

  (J) $x - 2 = 3$

  (K) $2(x - 3) = 4$

  (L) $\dfrac{x - 3}{2} = 1$

  (M) $3 - x = -1$

$$a^x \cdot a^y = a^{x+y}$$

3. Using the exponent property shown above, which of the following expression is equivalent to $2^4 \cdot 2^6$?

  (A) 2^{10}

  (B) 2^{12}

  (C) 2^{24}

  (D) 2^{46}

4. What is the value of $(x + 1)(x - 2)$ when $x = -2$?

  (J) -4

  (K) 2

  (L) 4

  (M) 6

5. A pencil costs $\$m$ and an eraser costs $\$n$. If Jason bought four erasers and two pencils, how much did he spend?

  (A) $4m + 2n$

  (B) $2m + 4n$

  (C) $4m + n$

  (D) $m + 2n$

6. If $x + y = 8$, what is the mean of x and y ?

  (J) 6

  (K) 5

  (L) 4

  (M) 2

7. Solve the equation: $\frac{1}{3}(x - 1) = 2$

(A) 7

(B) 6

(C) 5

(D) 4

[handwritten work:]
$\frac{1}{3}x - \frac{1}{3} = 2$
$+\frac{1}{3}$
$\frac{1}{3}x = 2\frac{1}{3}$
$x = 7$

8. A store is having a 20% off sale. If the regular price of a jacket was $\$k$, how much did Mr. Rhee pay with the discount?

(J) $1.2k$

(K) $0.8k$

(L) $0.6k$

(M) $0.2k$

[handwritten: Check]

9. 27 small identical cubes with side length of x are put together to form a larger cube. What is the length of the larger cube?

(A) $x + 3$

(B) $x + 27$

(C) $2x$

(D) $3x$

10. Solve the inequality: $1 - 2x < 5$

(J) $x > -2$

(K) $x > -3$

(L) $x < -2$

(M) $x < -3$

[handwritten work:]
$\frac{-2x}{-2} < \frac{4}{-2}$
$x > -2$

The product of two consecutive integers is 90.

11. Which of the following equation best represents verbal phrase above ? (Assuming that x be the smaller integer.)

(A) $x(x + 1) = 90$

(B) $x \cdot x + 1 = 90$

(C) $x \cdot 2x = 90$

(D) $x + x + 1 = 90$

12. if $x + 3 = y - 1 = 5$, then what is the value of $2xy$?

(J) 60

(K) 48

(L) 36

(M) 24

13. How many quarters are worth $\$n$?

(A) $2n$

(B) $4n$

(C) $5n$

(D) $15n$

14. If $x < 0$, what is the value of x for which $x^2 = 36$?

(J) -18

(K) -6

(L) 6

(M) 18

15. If one object makes one revolution, it rotates $360°$. Which of the following proportions can be used to find the measures of degree x that the object rotates if it makes 3 revolutions?

(A) $\dfrac{1}{360} = \dfrac{3}{x}$

(B) $\dfrac{1}{360} = \dfrac{x}{3}$

(C) $\dfrac{1}{3} = \dfrac{x}{360}$

(D) $\dfrac{1}{x} = \dfrac{360}{3}$

STOP

Answers and Solutions

IAAT Practice Test 3 Section 1

Answers

1. B	2. L	3. D	4. J	5. A
6. K	7. B	8. M	9. B	10. J
11. C	12. L	13. B	14. K	15. B

Solutions

1. (B)

   $0.31 \times 0.4 = 0.124$. Therefore, (B) is the correct answer.

2. (L)

   Joshua starts with the number 1 and counts by 4s. This results in the sequence: $1, 5, 9, 13, 17$, and 21. Thus, the 6th number in the sequence is 21. Therefore, (L) is the correct answer.

3. (D)

   $$\frac{2 \times 4 \times 6 \times 8}{1 \times 2 \times 3 \times 4} = \frac{2}{1} \times \frac{4}{2} \times \frac{6}{3} \times \frac{8}{4}$$
   $$= 2 \times 2 \times 2 \times 2$$
   $$= 16$$

   Therefore, (D) is the correct answer.

4. (J)

   Since $\dfrac{234}{9} = 26$,

   $$1 \text{ inch} = 9 \text{ miles} \qquad \text{Multiply both sides by 26}$$
   $$26 \text{ inches} = 234 \text{ miles}$$

   the distance that he drives on the map is 26 inches. Therefore, (J) is the correct answer.

5. (A)

   $$2\frac{1}{4} - \frac{5}{8} = \frac{9}{4} - \frac{5}{8} = \frac{18}{8} - \frac{5}{18}$$
   $$= \frac{13}{8} = 1\frac{5}{8}$$

   Therefore, (A) is the correct answer.

6. (K)

2 hours is equal to 120 minutes.

$$1 \text{ pancake} = 12 \text{ minutes}$$
$$10 \text{ pancakes} = 120 \text{ minutes}$$

Multiply both sides by 10

Therefore, (M) is the correct answer.

7. (B)

The business man paid 20% interest which means that he paid to the bank $0.2 \times \$500 = \$100$ for the interest. The total amount of money that the business man paid to the bank was the amount borrowed plus the interest which was $\$500 + \$100 = \$600$. Therefore, (B) is the correct answer.

8. (M)

$$\text{Multiple of } 2 = \{2, 4, 6, 8, 10, \mathbf{12}, \cdots\}$$
$$\text{Multiple of } 3 = \{3, 6, 9, \mathbf{12}, \cdots\}$$
$$\text{Multiple of } 4 = \{4, 8, \mathbf{12}, \cdots\}$$

Thus, the least common multiple (LCM) of 2, 3, and 4 is 12. Therefore, (M) is the correct answer.

9. (B)

$25\% = 0.25$, $\frac{1}{5} = 0.2$, and $\frac{1}{8} = 0.125$. Thus, $\{25\%, \frac{1}{5}, 0.15, \frac{1}{8}\}$ is ordered from greatest to least. Therefore, (B) is the correct answer.

10. (J)

The percent of the student in the school taking Spanish is $\dfrac{56}{200} = 0.28$ or 28%. Therefore, (J) is the correct answer.

11. (C)

Joshua ate $\frac{2}{3}$ of a pizza. So, the remaining pizza is $\dfrac{1}{3}$. After one hour, he ate $\frac{1}{3}$ of the remaining pizza which means that he ate $\frac{1}{3} \times \frac{1}{3} = \frac{1}{9}$. Thus, the fractional part of the pizza Joshua ate is $\frac{2}{3} + \frac{1}{9} = \frac{6}{9} + \frac{1}{9} = \frac{7}{9}$. Therefore, (C) is the correct answer.

12. (L)

$$23 + 45 + \square + 69 = 200$$
$$\square = 200 - 23 - 45 - 69$$
$$\square = 63$$

Therefore, (L) is the correct answer.

13. (B)

1 hour is equal to 60 minutes. Thus, 1 hour and 14 minutes is equal to $60 + 14$ or 74 minutes. Therefore, (B) is the correct answer.

14. (K)

Let x be age of Jason. Joshua is 7 years older than Jason can be expressed as $x + 7$. Sue is 23 years older than Jason can be expressed as $x + 23$. Thus, how much older than Joshua is Sue can be determined by $(x + 23) - (x + 7)$ or 16. Therefore, (K) is the correct answer.

15. (B)

Jason notices that he is the 12th person from the front of the line and is 11th person from the back of the line, which means there are 11 people in front of Jason and 10 people behind Jason. Thus, total number of people is $11 + 1(\text{Jason}) + 10$ or 22. Therefore, (B) is the correct answer.

Answers and Solutions

IAAT Practice Test 3 Section 2

Answers

1. A	2. L	3. B	4. K	5. A
6. M	7. D	8. K	9. A	10. K
11. B	12. L	13. D	14. M	15. A

Solutions

1. (A)

   Jason slept the most. Therefore, (A) is the correct answer.

2. (L)

   Joshua played the least. Therefore, (L) is the correct answer.

3. (B)

   Sue studied 3 hours. Therefore, (B) is the correct answer.

4. (K)

   Sue played 6 hours and Joshua played 2 hours. Thus, Sue played 4 hours more than Joshua. Therefore, (K) is the correct answer.

5. (A)

   The price of gasoline decrease most from July to August. Therefore, (A) is the correct answer.

6. (M)

   The price of gasoline in May is $2.7. Therefore, (M) is the correct answer.

7. (D)

$$\text{Percent increase} = \frac{\text{Final price-Initial price}}{\text{Initial price}} \times 100\%$$

   The price of gasoline in March is $2 and $3 in April. Thus, the percent increase of gasoline is $\frac{3-2}{2} \times 100\% = 50\%$. Therefore, (D) is the correct answer.

8. (K)

   The price of gasoline in July is $3.25 and the price of gasoline in June is $3. Thus, the price of the gasoline in July is $3.25 − $3 or $0.25 is higher than the price of gasoline in June. Therefore, (K) is the correct answer.

9. (A)

The percent of students named blue is $\dfrac{17}{50} = 0.34 = 34\%$. Therefore, (A) is the correct answer.

10. (K)

There are 15 students including Joshua and Jason in a row to get lunch. Joshua is the 7th from the front. Jason is 3rd from the back, which means that he is the 13th from the front. Thus, there are five students between Joshua and Jason: 8th, 9th, 10th, 11th, and 12th. Therefore, (K) is the correct answer.

11. (B)

The number of books sold on Wednesday is $189 - 22 - 52 - 17 - 33 = 65$. Therefore, (B) is the correct answer.

12. (L)

Four soccer teams A, B, C, and D compete against each other in a tournament. Each team plays against every other team only once. Let $A \leftrightarrow B$ represent team A competes against team B. The number of games played in all is 6:

$$A \leftrightarrow B, \quad A \leftrightarrow C, \quad A \leftrightarrow D, \quad B \leftrightarrow C, \quad B \leftrightarrow D \quad C \leftrightarrow D$$

Therefore, (L) is the correct answer.

13. (D)

2 pears and 2 apples weigh 24 ounces. Adding one more pear, 3 pears and 2 apples weigh 29 ounces. It means that the weight of one pear is $29 - 24 = 5$ ounces. Therefore, (D) is the correct answer.

14. (M)

Let x be the total number of students responded to Jason's survey. 18% of students surveyed can be expressed as $0.18x$, which is equal to 54. Thus, $0.18x = 54$. Solving for x gives $x = \frac{54}{0.18} = 300$. Therefore, (M) is the correct answer.

15. (A)

Mr. Rhee runs 90 miles in two weeks and runs 5 days a week. So, Mr. Rhee runs 90 miles in 10 days. Thus, the average number of miles Mr. Rhee run per day is $\frac{90}{10} = 9$. Therefore, (A) is the correct answer.

Answers and Solutions
IAAT Practice Test 3 Section 3

Answers

1. C	2. J	3. D	4. J	5. B
6. L	7. C	8. M	9. A	10. K
11. A	12. M	13. B	14. K	15. D

Solutions

1. (C)

   A car travels at 60 miles per hour which means that the car travels 60 miles in 60 minutes. Thus, the distance that the car travels in 30 minutes is $\frac{1}{2} \times 60 = 30$ miles. Therefore, (C) is the correct answer.

2. (J)

$$y = kx \qquad\qquad \text{Substitute } -3 \text{ for } k \text{ and } -2 \text{ for } x$$
$$y = (-3)(-2) = 6$$

   Therefore, (J) is the correct answer.

3. (D)

$$6 \text{ pancakes} = 6 \text{ eggs} + 3 \text{ cups of flour} \qquad \text{Multiply both side by } \frac{2}{3}$$
$$4 \text{ pancakes} = 4 \text{ eggs} + 2 \text{ cups of flour}$$

   Therefore, (D) is the correct answer.

4. (J)

   In a right triangle, the hypotenuse, side opposite the right angle, is c and other two sides are a and b. The square of the hypotenuse is equal to the sum of the squares of the other two sides can be defined as $c^2 = a^2 + b^2$. Therefore, (J) is the correct answer.

5. (B)

   Let x be the width of the rectangle. Since the perimeter P of the rectangle is 30, $P = 10+x+10+x = 30$ which gives $x = 5$. Thus, the area A of the rectangle is $A = \text{Length} \times \text{Width} = 10 \times 5 = 50$. Therefore, (B) is the correct answer.

6. (L)

The table in (L) contains ordered pairs $(3, 2)$, $(6, 3)$, and $(9, 6)$, which satisfy the equation $2x = 3y$. Therefore, (L) is the correct answer.

7. (C)

At 0 meter,	Pressure $= 10$
At 10 meter,	Pressure $= 10 + 15 = 25$
At 20 meter,	Pressure $= 25 + 15 = 40$
At 30 meter,	Pressure $= 40 + 15 = 55$
At 40 meter,	Pressure $= 55 + 15 = 70$
At 50 meter,	Pressure $= 70 + 15 = 85$

Therefore, (C) is the correct answer.

8. (M)

$V = \pi r^2 h$	Substitute 27π for V and 3 for r
$27\pi = \pi(3^2)h$	Divide both sides by 9π
$h = 3$	

Thus, the height of the cylinder is 3. Therefore, (M) is the correct answer.

9. (A)

The range is a set of y-values. Thus, the range is $\{2, 6, 7, 9\}$. Therefore, (A) is the correct answer.

10. (K)

When the x-value is given, the corresponding y-value is 20 times larger than the x-value, which can be expressed as $y = 20x$. Therefore, (K) is the correct answer.

11. (A)

The table contains ordered pairs $(-2, 0)$, $(0, 2)$, and $(1, 3)$. If you plot these ordered pairs and connect them, you get a straight line shown in (A). Therefore, (A) is the correct answer.

12. (M)

The definition of slope is rise over run. x increases by 1 and y decreases by 2 means that rise is -2 and run is 1. Thus, slope $= \frac{\text{rise}}{\text{run}} = \frac{-2}{1} = -2$. Since the equation $y = -2x - 1$ has a slope of -2, (M) is the correct answer.

13. (B)

Substituting 2 and 4 for x in $y = \frac{1}{2}x - 3$ gives -2 and -1 for y, respectively. It means that the table contains ordered pairs $(2, -2)$ and $(4, -1)$. Since the table in (B) contains the ordered pairs $(2, -2)$ and $(4, -1)$, (B) is the correct answer.

14. (K)

> $y = 3$ represents the line given, which means that y-values are always 3 no matter what values of x are given. Since the table in (K) has y-values equal to 3, (K) is the correct answer.

15. (D)

> In order to find the area A of the Trapezoid, take the sum of its bases, multiply the sum by the height of the trapezoid, and then divide the result by 2. Thus, $A = \frac{1}{2}(b_1 + b_2)h$. Therefore, (D) is the correct answer.

Answers and Solutions

IAAT Practice Test 3 Section 4

Answers

1. D	2. M	3. A	4. L	5. B
6. L	7. A	8. K	9. D	10. J
11. A	12. M	13. B	14. K	15. A

Solutions

1. (D)

   Joshua is x years old now. In 10 years ago, he was $x - 10$ years old. Therefore, (D) is the correct answer.

2. (M)

   Multiplying both sides of the equation $x - 3 = 2$ gives $3 - x = -2$. Thus, $3 - x = -1$ is false. Therefore, (M) is the correct answer.

3. (A)

   According to the exponent property $a^x \cdot a^y = a^{x+y}$, $2^4 \cdot 2^6 = 2^{4+6} = 2^{10}$. Therefore, (A) is the correct answer.

4. (L)

   Substituting -2 for x in $(x+1)(x-2)$ gives $(-2+1)(-2-2) = 4$. Therefore, (L) is the correct answer.

5. (B)

   A pencil costs \$$m$ and an eraser costs \$$n$. If Jason bought four erasers and two pencils, he spent $4n + 2m$ or $2m + 4n$. Therefore, (B) is the correct answer.

6. (L)

   $x + y = 8$. The mean of x and y is $\frac{x+y}{2} = \frac{8}{2} = 4$. Therefore, (L) is the correct answer.

7. (A)

$$\frac{1}{3}(x - 1) = 2 \qquad \text{Multiply both sides by 3}$$
$$x - 1 = 6 \qquad \text{Add 1 to both sides}$$
$$x = 7$$

   Therefore, (A) is the correct answer.

8. (K)

A store is having a 20% off sale. If the regular price of a jacket was k, Mr. Rhee paid 80% of the regular price of the jacket, which is $80\% \times k$ or $0.8k$. Therefore, (K) is the correct answer.

9. (D)

The volume of each smaller cube with side length of x is x^3. So, the volume of 27 identical smaller cubes with side length of x is $27x^3$. 27 small identical cubes are put together to form a larger cube. Let y be the length of the larger cube. Since the volume of the larger cube must be equal to the volume of 27 smaller cubes, $y^3 = 27x^3$, which gives $y = 3x$. Thus, the length of the larger cube is $3x$. Therefore, (D) is the correct answer.

10. (J)

$$1 - 2x < 5 \qquad \text{Subtract 1 from both sides}$$
$$-2x < 4 \qquad \text{Divide both sides by } -2$$
$$x > -2 \qquad \text{Reverse the inequality symbol}$$

Therefore, (J) is the correct answer.

11. (A)

Let x be the smaller integer. $x + 1$ is a consecutive integer. Thus, the product of two consecutive integers is 90 can be defined as $x(x + 1) = 90$. Therefore, (A) is the correct answer.

12. (M)

$x + 3 = 5$ gives $x = 2$. $y - 1 = 5$ gives $y = 6$. Thus, $2xy = 2(2)(6) = 24$. Therefore, (M) is the correct answer.

13. (B)

A quarter is worth 25 cents. So, 4 quarter is worth 100 cents or $1.

$$\$1 = 4 \text{ quarters} \qquad \text{Multiply both sides by } n$$
$$\$n = 4n \text{ quarters}$$

Therefore, (B) is the correct answer.

14. (K)

The values of x for which $x^2 = 36$ are either $x = 6$ or $x = -6$. Since $x < 0$, $x = -6$. Therefore, (K) is the correct answer.

15. (A)

Set up an proportion: $\dfrac{\text{Revolution}}{\text{Degree}} = \dfrac{1}{360°} = \dfrac{3}{x°}$. Therefore, (A) is the correct answer.

IAAT PRACTICE TEST 4

SECTION 1
Time — 10 minutes
15 Questions

Directions: Read the information given and choose the best answer for each question. Base your answer only on the information given. The time limit for each section is 10 minutes.

1. Evaluate $0.25 + \dfrac{3}{8}$.

   (A) 0.375

   (B) 0.425

   (C) 0.575

   (D) 0.625

2. Round 0.23785 to the nearest thousandth.

   (J) 0.2379

   (K) 0.238

   (L) 0.24

   (M) 0.2

3. Joshua spent $49 on a pair of jeans. If he has left $375 on his savings account, how much money was in his savings account in the beginning?

   (A) $424

   (B) $414

   (C) $336

   (D) $326

4. Which of the following numbers have only two factors?

   (J) 12

   (K) 24

   (L) 31

   (M) 44

5. $\dfrac{1}{3}(9)^2 - \sqrt{16} \div 2 =$

   (A) 1

   (B) 5

   (C) 10

   (D) 25

6. Which of the following number has the largest remainder when the number is divided by 7?

   (J) 45

   (K) 46

   (L) 47

   (M) 48

7. Which of the following number is NOT equivalent to the other three?

(A) $\dfrac{2}{5}$

(B) 4×10^{-2}

(C) 0.4

(D) $\dfrac{8}{20}$

8. $\begin{bmatrix} 1 & 3 \\ 4 & 2 \end{bmatrix} + \begin{bmatrix} 4 & 1 \\ 2 & 3 \end{bmatrix} =$

(J) $\begin{bmatrix} 4 & 3 \\ 8 & 6 \end{bmatrix}$

(K) $\begin{bmatrix} 5 & 4 \\ 6 & 5 \end{bmatrix}$

(L) $\begin{bmatrix} 5 & 6 \\ 4 & 5 \end{bmatrix}$

(M) $\begin{bmatrix} 3 & 2 \\ 2 & 1 \end{bmatrix}$

9. Which of the following expression has the least value?

(A) $1 \cdot 2 \cdot 3$

(B) $2 \cdot 3 \cdot 4$

(C) $3 \cdot 4 \cdot 5$

(D) $4 \cdot 5 \cdot 6$

10. A recent basketball statistics indicates that Jason has a 75% free throw shooting average. Based on the statistics, how many free throws will Jason make if he attempts 12 free throws?

(J) 9

(K) 8

(L) 7

(M) 6

11. Which of the following expression has the largest value ?

(A) $\sqrt{12}$

(B) $\sqrt{14}$

(C) $\sqrt{16}$

(D) $\sqrt{18}$

12. The sales tax rate is 6%. If Joshua buys a bicycle for $125, what is the amount of tax that he must pay?

(J) $7.50

(K) $8.75

(L) $10.50

(M) $12.25

13. Which quadrant of a coordinate plane is the ordered pair $(-2, 5)$ located?

    (A) I

    (B) II

    (C) III

    (D) IV

14. How many seconds is equivalent to 5.3 minutes?

    (J) 310 seconds

    (K) 318 seconds

    (L) 330 seconds

    (M) 350 seconds

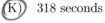

300

$\begin{array}{r} 60 \\ \underline{13} \\ 180 \end{array}$

15. A nickel and a dime are in a bag. Each of three students selects one coin from the bag and put it back again for the next student. Which of the following expressions represent the total number of ways that three students select coins?

    (A) 2×2

    (B) 2×3

    (C) 3×3

    (D) $2 \times 2 \times 2$

14/15

STOP

IAAT PRACTICE TEST 4

SECTION 2
Time — 10 minutes
15 Questions

Directions: Read the information given and choose the best answer for each question. Base your answer only on the information given. The time limit for each section is 10 minutes.

Directions: Two box-and-whisker plots shown below show the distribution of math scores in class A and class B. Use the box-and-whisker plots to answer questions 1 − 4.

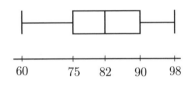

60   75   82   90   98

Class A

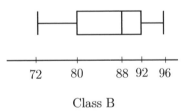

72   80   88 92   96

Class B

1. What is the median math score in class A?

(A)   88

(B)   86

(C)   85

(D)   82

2. What is the range of math scores in class A?

(J)   42

(K)   38

(L)   26

(M)   22

3. What is the difference between the upper extreme of class A and that of class B?

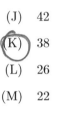

(A)   2

(B)   5

(C)   8

(D)   12

4. The interquartile range (IQR) is upper quartile minus lower quartile. In the box-and-whisker plot of class A, upper quartile is 90 and lower quartile is 75 so that IQR = 15. What is the interquartile range of class B?

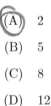

(J)   24

(K)   20

(L)   18

(M)   12

Directions: A rectangular tank with length of 2 cm, width of 4 cm, and height of 6 cm is shown below. Use the rectangular tank to answer questions 5 – 8.

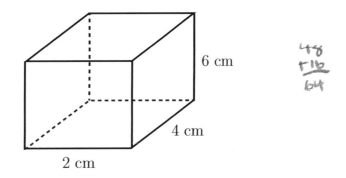

A rectangular tank

5. What is the volume of the rectangular tank?

   (A) 48 cm^3

   (B) 36 cm^3

   (C) 24 cm^3

   (D) 12 cm^3

6. What is the area of the base of the rectangular tank?

   (J)   24 cm^2

   (K) 20 cm^2

   (L) 12 cm^2

   (M) 8 cm^2

7. If Jason wants to cover the rectangular tank with paper, what is the amount of paper that Jason needs?

   (A) 42 cm^2

   (B) 64 cm^2

   (C) 88 cm^2

   (D) 96 cm^2

8. If water is being pumped into the rectangular tank at a rate of 8 cm^3/min, how long it will take to fill the tank with water ?

   (J)   6 minutes

   (K) 8 minutes

   (L) 10 minutes

   (M) 12 minutes

9. Which of the following scatter plots contain data with a positive relationship?

Check

(A)

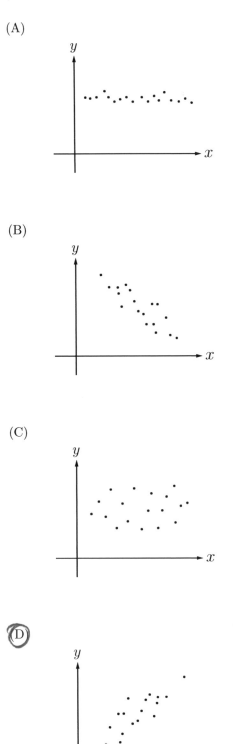

(B)

(C)

(D)

Directions: Use the following diagram to answer question 10-11.

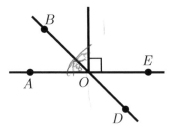

10. If the measure of $\angle AOB = 40°$, what is the measure of $\angle BOE$?

    (J)   150°

    (K)   140°

    (L)   120°

    (M)   110°

11. If the measure of $\angle AOB = 40°$, what is the measure of $\angle DOE$?

    (A)   30°

    (B)   40°

    (C)   50°

    (D)   60°

Directions: Use the following number line to answer questions 12 − 14.

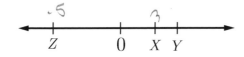

12. If $X = 3$ and $Z = -5$, what is the value of $X - Z$?

    (J) 8

    (K) 2

    (L) −2

    (M) −8

13. Which of the following expression has the largest value?

    (A) $X - Z$

    (B) $Y - Z$

    (C) $Y - X$

    (D) $Z - Y$

14. The distance between Y and 0 is twice as long the distance between Z and 0, what is the value of Z if $Y = 6$?

    (J) −5

    (K) −3

    (L) 3

    (M) 5

15. A clock indicates 9:00 AM. What is the measure of an angle formed by an hour hand and a minute hand?

    (A) 120°

    (B) 90°

    (C) 60°

    (D) 45°

101   www.solomonacademy.net

IAAT PRACTICE TEST 4

SECTION 3

Time — 10 minutes

15 Questions

Directions: Read the information given and choose the best answer for each question. Base your answer only on the information given. The time limit for each section is 10 minutes.

1. A telephone company charges a monthly fee of $25 in addition to 10 cents per minute. If a customer used t minutes in March, how much, in dollars, would the telephone company charge the customer?

    (A) $35t$

    (B) $25t + 10$

    (C) $25 + 0.1t$

    (D) $25 + 10t$

2. If $x = \dfrac{12}{y}$, what is the value of y when $x = 3$?

    (J)   36

    (K)   12

    (L)   6

    (M)   4

y	2	4	6	8
x	2	3	4	5

3. The table above shows four pairs of x and y values. Which of the following equation is true for all values in the table?

    (A) $x = y$

    (B) $x = y + 2$

    (C) $x = \dfrac{1}{2}y + 1$

    (D) $x = \dfrac{1}{2}y - 1$

4. Which ordered pair satisfies the inequality $x > 7 - y$?

    (J) $(2, 6)$

    (K) $(3, 3)$

    (L) $(4, 3)$

    (M) $(5, 1)$

www.solomonacademy.net

5. Mode is a number that is shown most frequently in a set of data. What is the mode of the data shown below?

$$\{5, 9, 8, 6, 9, 10, 13, 7\}$$

(A)   13

(B)   9

(C)   8

(D)   5

6. Ohm's law states that $V = I \times R$, where V is voltage in volts, I is current in amps, and R is resistance in ohms. Suppose a current, I, of 2 amps flows through a resistor. If the voltage, V, is 12 volts, what is the resistance, R, of the resistor?

(J)   24 ohms

(K)   12 ohms

(L)   6 ohms

(M)   3 ohms

7. Which of the following equation best represents the following verbal relationship? The ratio of y and x is 3.

(A) $x + y = 3$

(B) $xy = 3$

(C) $\frac{x}{y} = 3$

(D) $\frac{y}{x} = 3$

Input	Output
1	1
2	4
⋮	⋮
7	
⋮	⋮
10	100

8. Observe the numbers in the two columns shown above. Which of the following value should be in the empty cell?

(J)   14

(K)   19

(L)   35

(M)   49

9. Which of the following table contains some ordered pairs that do NOT satisfy the equation, $y = x + 5$?

(A)

x	-5	-4	-3	-2
y	0	1	2	3

(B)

x	-3	-2	-1	0
y	2	1	0	-1

(C)

x	-2	-1	0	1
y	3	4	5	6

(D)

x	0	1	2	3
y	5	6	7	8

Month	February	March	April	May
Change	−$150	$400	$200	−$300

10. Jason has an unknown balance in his savings account at the end of January. The table above shows the change in his balance comparing with the balance in previous month over four months. If Jason's balance at the end of May is $1000, then what was his balance at the end of January?

(J) $1150

(K) $950

(L) $850

(M) $750

11. If $x > 0$, $y < 0$, and $z < 0$, which of the following inequality is NOT true?

(A) $yz < 0$

(B) $xy < 0$

(C) $xz < 0$

(D) $\dfrac{x}{z} < 0$

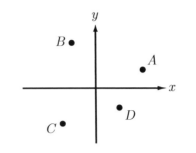

12. Which of the following lettered point best represents an ordered pair $(-1, 3)$?

(J) A

(K) B

(L) C

(M) D

13. Which of the following table best represents the following verbal relationship? The number of TVs sold, x, is twice as many as the number of DVDs sold, y.

(A)

x	100	200	300	400
y	100	200	300	400

(B)

x	100	200	300	400
y	50	100	200	400

(C)

x	100	200	300	400
y	200	400	600	800

(D)

x	100	200	300	400
y	50	100	150	200

Year	Number Sold
1	385
2	461
3	423
4	411
5	474

14. The table above shows the number of girl scout cookies sold over 5 years. What is the median number of girl scout cookies sold per year?

   (J)   461 cookies

   (K)   423 cookies

   (L)   411 cookies

   (M)   385 cookies

15. A car dealership has 200 cars in its inventory. Of which

- 30% cars are black.
- 40 are blue.
- 80 cars are white.
- 10% are red.

If you buy a car from the dealership, what is the probability that the car you buy is either black or white?

(A) $\dfrac{90}{200}$

(B) $\dfrac{110}{200}$

(C) $\dfrac{140}{200}$

(D) $\dfrac{150}{200}$

STOP

IAAT PRACTICE TEST 4

SECTION 4
Time — 10 minutes
15 Questions

Directions: Read the information given and choose the best answer for each question. Base your answer only on the information given. The time limit for each section is 10 minutes.

Three-fourth of y is 8.

1. Which of the following equation represents the verbal phrase above?

   (A) $\dfrac{3}{4}y = 8$

   (B) $\dfrac{3}{y} = 8$

   (C) $3y = 8$

   (D) $0.3y = 8$

---

2. If $a\bigstar b = b^a$, what is the value of $2\bigstar 3$?

   (J) 3

   (K) 6

   (L) 8

   (M) 9

---

3. Find the value of x that satisfies the equation $3(x+1) = 5(x+1)$?

   (A) 2

   (B) 0

   (C) −1

   (D) −3

---

4. If $\dfrac{10}{x} = y$, what is x in terms of y ?

   (J) $x = \dfrac{10}{y}$

   (K) $x = \dfrac{y}{10}$

   (L) $x = 10y$

   (M) $x = 10 - y$

---

5. Joshua bought a large box which contains 6 smaller boxes of cereal at wholesale store. If Joshua paid \$12.99 for the large box, and wants to make a \$1 profit on each smaller box when he sell it, which expression best represents P, the price of the smaller box of cereal?

   (A) $P = \dfrac{12.99 + 1}{6}$

   (B) $P = \dfrac{12.99 - 1}{6}$

   (C) $P = \dfrac{12.99}{6} - 1$

   (D) $P = \dfrac{12.99}{6} + 1$

         www.solomonacademy.net

6. Which phrase best represents $\frac{x}{2} + 3$?

  (J)   The product of a number and 3 divided by 2

  (K)   The sum of x and 3 divided by 2

  (L)   Three added to the quotient of a number and 2

  (M)   Three added to the quotient of 2 and a number

7. A train is 10 miles due East of a station. If the train travels due East at a rate of 65 miles per hour, how many miles would it be away from the station in t hours?

  (A) $65t$

  (B) $10 + 65t$

  (C) $75t$

  (D) $75t + 10$

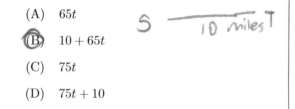

8. What is the value of y that makes the equation true ?

$$\sqrt{x+y} = \sqrt{x}$$

  (J)   0

  (K)   1

  (L)   4

  (M)   9

9. Simplify the expression $a - b + c + b - a - c$.

  (A) $2a + 2b + 2c$

  (B) $2a + b$

  (C) $2c$

  (D)   0

10. If $2^6 = 4^x$, what is the value of x ?

  (J)   0

  (K)   1

  (L)   2

  (M)   3

11. The price of a stock in January was unknown. If the price of stock is quadrupled so that the price is $3k$, what is the price of the stock in January ?

  (A) $\frac{3k}{4}$

  (B) $\frac{3k}{2}$

  (C) $9k$

  (D) $12k$

Check

12. The area, A, of an equilateral triangle with side length S is given by $A = \frac{\sqrt{3}}{4}S^2$. What is the area of an equilateral triangle with side length 10 ?

  (J) $25\sqrt{3}$

  (K) $50\sqrt{3}$

  (L) $75\sqrt{3}$

  (M) $100\sqrt{3}$

13. If $\sqrt{40} < n < \sqrt{60}$ and n is a positive integer, what is the value of n ?

    (A)   5

    (B)   6

    (C)   7

    (D)   8

---

14. The factorial of a non-negative integer n, denoted by n!, is the product of all positive integers less than or equal to n. For instance, $3! = 3 \times 2 \times 1 = 6$. Which of the following expression is equivalent to $4! \times 5$?

    (J) 9!

    (K) 7!

    (L) 6!

    (M) 5!

15. Let M and m be the greatest value and the smallest value of a data set, respectively. For instance, in the data set $\{2, 5, 6, 9\}$, $M = 9$ and $m = 2$. What is the sum of M and m of the following data set $\{8, 3, 9, 2, 11, 6\}$?

    (A)   16

    (B)   14

    (C)   13

    (D)   11

STOP

Answers and Solutions

IAAT Practice Test 4 Section 1

Answers

1. D	2. K	3. A	4. L	5. D
6. M	7. B	8. K	9. A	10. J
11. D	12. J	13. B	14. K	15. D

Solutions

1. (D)

   $0.25 + \dfrac{3}{8} = 0.25 + 0.375 = 0.625$. Therefore, (D) is the correct answer.

2. (K)

   Rounding 0.23785 to the nearest thousandth gives 0.238. Therefore, (K) is the correct answer.

3. (A)

   Let x be the amount of money in his savings account in the beginning. Joshua spent \$49 on a pair of jeans and he has left \$375 on his savings account, which can be expressed as $x - 49 = 375$. Thus, $x = 375 + 49 = 424$. Therefore, (A) is the correct answer.

4. (L)

   A prime number has only two factors. Among answer choices, 31 is a prime number. Therefore, (L) is the correct answer.

5. (D)

$$\frac{1}{3}(9)^2 - \sqrt{16} \div 2 = \frac{1}{3}(81) - 4 \div 2$$
$$= 27 - 2$$
$$= 25$$

   Therefore, (D) is the correct answer.

6. (M)

   When 48 is divided by 7, the remainder is 6, which is the largest remainder among answer choices. Therefore, (M) is the correct answer.

7. (B)

   $\frac{8}{20} = \frac{2}{5} = 0.4$. $4 \times 10^{-2} = 0.04$ is not equivalent to other three. Therefore, (B) is the correct answer.

8. (K)

Addition of two matrices is done entry-wise. $\begin{bmatrix} 1 & 3 \\ 4 & 2 \end{bmatrix} + \begin{bmatrix} 4 & 1 \\ 2 & 3 \end{bmatrix} = \begin{bmatrix} 1+4 & 3+1 \\ 4+2 & 2+3 \end{bmatrix} = \begin{bmatrix} 5 & 4 \\ 6 & 5 \end{bmatrix}$

Therefore, (K) is the correct answer.

9. (A)

$1 \cdot 2 \cdot 3 = 6$, which is the least value among answer choice. Therefore, (A) is the correct answer.

10. (J)

$75\% = \frac{3}{4}$. The number of free throws will Jason make if he attempts 12 free throws is $12 \times \frac{3}{4} = 9$. Therefore, (J) is the correct answer.

11. (D)

The larger the value inside the square root, the larger the value of the square root. Therefore, (D) is the correct answer.

12. (J)

Joshua buys a bicycle for \$125 and the sales tax rate is 6%. Thus, the amount of tax that Joshua must pay is $125 \times 0.06 = 7.5$. Therefore, (J) is the correct answer.

13. (B)

The ordered pair $(-2, 5)$ is located in the second quadrant as shown below.

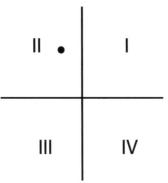

Therefore, (B) is the correct answer.

14. (K)

1 minute is equal 60 seconds. Thus, 5.3 minutes is equal to 5.3×60 or 318 seconds. Therefore, (K) is the correct answer.

15. (D)

Each student has two ways to select a coin: either a nickel or a dime. Thus, the expression that represents the total number of ways that three students select coins is $2 \times 2 \times 2$. Therefore, (D) is the correct answer.

Answers and Solutions
IAAT Practice Test 4 Section 2

Answers

1. D	2. K	3. A	4. M	5. A
6. M	7. C	8. J	9. D	10. K
11. B	12. J	13. B	14. K	15. B

Solutions

1. (D)

   A line inside the box represents the median math score, which is 82. Therefore, (D) is the correct answer.

2. (K)

   The range is the difference of the largest number and the smallest number. Thus, the range of math scores in class A is $98 - 60 = 38$. Therefore, (K) is the correct answer.

3. (A)

   The upper extreme of class A is 98 and the upper extreme of class B is 96. Thus, the difference of two extremes is $98 - 96 = 2$. Therefore, (A) is the correct answer.

4. (M)

   The upper quartile of class B is 92 and lower quartile of class B is 80 so that IQR $= 92 - 80 = 12$. Therefore, (M) is the correct answer.

5. (A)

   The volume V of a rectangular box is $V = $ Length $\times$ Width $\times$ Height. Thus, the volume of the rectangular tank is $2 \times 4 \times 6 = 48$. Therefore, (A) is the correct answer.

6. (M)

   The area of the base of the rectangular tank is $2 \times 4 = 8$. Therefore, (M) is the correct answer.

7. (C)

   The surface area of the rectangular tank is the sum of areas of six faces. The areas of the top and bottom faces are $2 \times 4 = 8$ each. The areas of the left and right faces are $4 \times 6 = 24$ each. The areas of the front and back faces are $2 \times 6 = 12$ each. Thus, the surface area of the rectangular tank is $8 + 8 + 24 + 24 + 12 + 12 = 88$. Therefore, (C) is the correct answer.

8. (J)

The volume of the rectangular tank is 48 cm^3. Since water is being pumped into the rectangular tank at a rate of 8 cm^3/min, it will take $\frac{48}{8}$ or 6 minutes to fill the tank with water. Therefore, (J) is the correct answer.

9. (D)

The scatter plot with a positive relationship shows that y increases as x increases. Thus, the scatter plot in (D) best represents the relationship. Therefore, (D) is the correct answer.

10. (K)

A straight line AE has 180°. Since the measure of $\angle AOB = 40°$, the measure of $\angle BOE$ is $180° - 40° = 140°$. Therefore, (K) is the correct answer.

11. (B)

Two angles $\angle AOB$ and $\angle DOE$ are vertical angles whose measures are the same. Thus, the measure of $\angle DOE = 40°$. Therefore, (B) is the correct answer.

12. (J)

Since $X = 3$ and $Z = -5$, the value of $X - Z$ is $3 - (-5) = 8$. Therefore, (J) is the correct answer.

13. (B)

$Y - Z$ represents the distance between Y and Z. Since Y and Z are the furthest apart points, the expression $Y - Z$ has the largest value. Therefore, (C) is the correct answer.

14. (K)

If $Y = 6$, the distance between Y and 0 is 6, which is twice as long the distance between Z and 0. So, the distance between Z and 0 is 3, which implies that $z = -3$. Therefore, (K) is the correct answer.

15. (B)

If a clock indicates 9:00 AM, the measure of an angle formed by an hour hand and a minute hand is exactly 90°. Therefore, (B) is the correct answer.

Answers and Solutions

IAAT Practice Test 4 Section 3

Answers

1. C	2. M	3. C	4. J	5. B
6. L	7. D	8. M	9. B	10. L
11. A	12. K	13. D	14. K	15. C

Solutions

1. **(C)**

   If a customer used t minutes, he or she would pay $\$0.1 \times t$ in addition to a monthly fee of $\$25$, which can be expressed as $25 + 0.1t$. Therefore, (C) is the correct answer.

2. **(M)**

   Substituting 3 for x in $x = \dfrac{12}{y}$ gives $3 = \dfrac{12}{y}$. So, $y = 4$. Therefore, (M) is the correct answer.

3. **(C)**

   The table shows a relationship such that the values of x is 1 more than half the values of y, which can be defined as $x = \dfrac{1}{2}y + 1$. Therefore, (C) is the correct answer.

4. **(J)**

   When substituting 2 for x and 6 for y in $x > 7 - y$,

$x > 7 - y$	Substituting 2 for x and 6 for y
$2 > 7 - 6$	Simplify
$2 > 1$	True

   $2 > 1$ is true. Thus, $(2, 6)$ is an ordered pair that satisfies the inequality $x > 7 - y$. Therefore, (J) is the correct answer.

5. **(B)**

   9 is a number that is shown most frequently in a set of data. Thus, the mode of the data is 9. Therefore, (B) is the correct answer.

6. (L)

Substitute 12 for V and 2 for I in $V = I \times R$.

$$V = I \times R \qquad \text{Substitute 12 for } V \text{ and 2 for } I$$
$$2 \times R = 12 \qquad \text{Divide both sides by 2}$$
$$R = 6$$

the resistance, R, of the resistor is 6 ohms. Therefore, (L) is the correct answer.

7. (D)

The ratio of y and x is 3 can be expressed as $\dfrac{y}{x} = 3$. Therefore, (D) is the correct answer.

8. (M)

The table shows a relationship such that output = input^2. When input = 7, output = $7^2 = 49$. Thus, the value in the empty cell is 49. Therefore, (M) is the correct answer.

9. (B)

The table in (B) does not satisfies the equation, $y = x + 5$. For instance, substituting -2 for x and 1 for y in $y = x + 5$ gives $1 \neq -2 + 5$. Therefore, (B) is the correct answer.

10. (L)

Let x be Jason's balance at the end of January. Then, Jason's balance at the end of February can be defined as $x - 150$ and Jason's balance at the end of March can be defined as $x - 150 + 400$, or $x + 250$. Since Jason's balance at the end of May can be defined $x - 150 + 400 + 200 - 300$ or $x + 150$ and is equal to 1000, $x + 150 = 1000$ which gives $x = 850$. Therefore, (L) is the correct answer.

11. (A)

$x > 0$, $y < 0$, and $z < 0$ indicates that x is a positive number, y and z are both negative numbers. Since the product of two negative numbers is a positive number, $yz > 0$. Therefore, (A) is the correct answer.

12. (K)

The ordered pair $(-1, 3)$ indicates that $x = -1$ and $y = 3$. Since $(-1, 3)$ is located at the second quadrant, B best represents the ordered pair $(-1, 3)$. Therefore, (K) is the correct answer.

13. (D)

The number of TVs sold, x, is twice as many as the number of DVDs sold, y can be expressed as $x = 2y$. The table in (D) shows a relationship $x = 2y$. Therefore, (D) is the correct answer.

14. (K)

Arrange the numbers from least to greatest: $\{385, 411, 423, 461, 474\}$
The median is the middle number of the data set. Thus, the median number of girl scout cookies sold per year is 423. Therefore, (K) is the correct answer.

15. (C)

A car dealership has 200 cars in its inventory. Out of 200 cars, 30% of 200 cars or $0.3 \times 200 = 60$ are black and 80 cars are white. the probability that the car you buy is either black or white is $\frac{60}{200} + \frac{80}{200} = \frac{140}{200}$. Therefore, (C) is the correct answer.

Answers and Solutions

IAAT Practice Test 4 Section 4

Answers

1. A	2. M	3. C	4. J	5. D
6. L	7. B	8. J	9. D	10. M
11. A	12. J	13. C	14. M	15. C

Solutions

1. (A)

   Three-fourth of y is 8 can be expressed as $\dfrac{3}{4}y = 8$. Therefore, (A) is the correct answer.

2. (M)

   $a \bigstar b = b^a$, Thus, the value of $2 \bigstar 3 = 3^2 = 9$. Therefore, (M) is the correct answer.

3. (C)

$3(x + 1) = 5(x + 1)$	Use the distributive property: $a(b + c) = ab + ac$
$5x + 5 = 3x + 3$	Subtract $3x$ from both sides
$2x + 5 = 3$	Subtract 5 from both sides
$2x = -2$	Divide both sides by 2
$x = -1$	

   Therefore, (C) is the correct answer.

4. (J)

$\dfrac{10}{x} = y$	Multiply both sides by x
$xy = 10$	Divide both sides by y
$x = \dfrac{10}{y}$	

   Therefore, (J) is the correct answer.

5. (D)

Joshua paid \$12.99 for a large box which contains 6 smaller boxes of cereal. It means that the cost of one smaller box of cereal is $\dfrac{12.99}{6}$. Since Joshua wants to make a \$1 profit on each smaller box when he sell it, the price of the smaller box of cereal should be $\dfrac{12.99}{6} + 1$. Therefore, (D) is the correct answer.

6. (L)

$\dfrac{x}{2} + 3$ means that three added to the quotient of a number and 2. Therefore, (L) is the correct answer.

7. (B)

The train travels at a rate of 65 miles per hour means that the train travels 65 miles in 1 hour. So, the train is away from the station $10 + 65$ or 75 miles in 1 hour, $10 + 65(2)$ or 140 miles in 2 hours, and $10 + 65(3)$ or 205 miles in 3 hours. Thus, the train is away from the station in t hours can be expressed as $10 + 65t$ miles. Therefore, (B) is the correct answer.

8. (J)

The only value of y that makes the equation $\sqrt{x+y} = \sqrt{x}$ true is 0. Therefore, (J) is the correct answer.

9. (D)

$a - b + c + b - a - c = (a - a) + (-b + b) + (c - c) = 0$. Therefore, (D) is the correct answer.

10. (M)

Since $2^6 = 64$ and $4^3 = 64$, the value of x is 3. Therefore, (M) is the correct answer.

11. (A)

Let x be the price of a stock in January. The price of stock is quadrupled so that the price is $3k$ can be expressed as $x \times 4 = 3k$ which gives $x = \dfrac{3k}{4}$. Therefore, (A) is the correct answer.

12. (J)

$A = \dfrac{\sqrt{3}}{4} S^2 = \dfrac{\sqrt{3}}{4} (10)^2 = 25\sqrt{3}$. Therefore, (J) is the correct answer.

13. (C)

$$\sqrt{40} < n < \sqrt{60} \qquad \text{Square each side}$$
$$40 < n^2 < 60$$

Since $7^2 = 49$, $n = 7$ satisfies $40 < n^2 < 60$. Therefore, (C) is the correct answer.

14. (M)

$$4! \times 5 = 5 \times 4! = 5 \times 4 \times 3 \times 2 \times 1 = 5!$$

Therefore, (M) is the correct answer.

15. (C)

From the data set $\{8, 3, 9, 2, 11, 6\}$, $M = 11$ and $m = 2$. The sum of M and m is $11 + 2 = 13$. Therefore, (C) is the correct answer.

IAAT PRACTICE TEST 5

SECTION 1
Time — 10 minutes
15 Questions

Directions: Read the information given and choose the best answer for each question. Base your answer only on the information given. The time limit for each section is 10 minutes.

1. What is the dimension of the matrix shown below?

$$\begin{bmatrix} 2 & 1 & 4 \\ -1 & 3 & 2 \end{bmatrix}$$

(A) 3 by 2

(B) 2 by 3

(C) 1 by 6

(D) 6 by 1

2. 1 ton is equal to 2000 pounds. How many pounds is equal to 1.5 tons?

(J) 800 pounds

(K) 1500 pounds

(L) 3000 pounds

(M) 4500 pounds

3. $1.24 + 0.86 + 2.1 =$

(A) 4.2

(B) 4.1

(C) 4.0

(D) 3.9

4. If there are seven quarters, three dimes, and two nickels in a coin purse, what is the total amount of money in the coin purse?

(J) $2.35

(K) $2.25

(L) $2.15

(M) $2.05

5. All numbers have only 2 factors EXCEPT

(A) 7

(B) 8

(C) 11

(D) 13

6. The sum of four numbers is 240. If 10 is added, what is the average of the five numbers?

(J) 45

(K) 50

(L) 55

(M) 60

7. How many minutes are there in 5.4 hours? (1 hour=60 minutes)

   (A)   540 minutes

   (B)   424 minutes

   (C)   340 minutes

   (D)   324 minutes

8. $\dfrac{25}{3} \div \dfrac{3}{4} =$

   (J) $\dfrac{100}{9}$

   (K) $\dfrac{100}{12}$

   (L) $\dfrac{75}{9}$

   (M) $\dfrac{75}{12}$

9. Joshua walks due West at a rate of 3 ft/s. Jason walks due East at a rate of 2 ft/s. How many feet are they apart in 7 seconds?

   (A)   7 feet

   (B)   24 feet

   (C)   35 feet

   (D)   42 feet

10.   If $\pi = 3.14$, what is the value of 8π ?

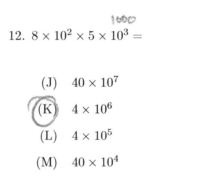

   (J)   24.02

   (K)   24.12

   (L)   25.02

   (M)   25.12

11. Which of the following is NOT equal to other three?

   (A)   40%

   (B)   0.4

   (C) $\dfrac{2}{5}$

   (D) $\dfrac{1}{40}$

12. $8 \times 10^2 \times 5 \times 10^3 =$

   (J) 40×10^7

   (K) 4×10^6

   (L) 4×10^5

   (M) 40×10^4

$$4 \,\square\, 3 \,\triangle\, 2 = 10$$

13. Each $\square$ and $\triangle$ shown above represents one of the basic arithmetic operators: $+$, $-$, $\times$, and $\div$. Which of the following best represents $\square$ and $\triangle$?

   (A) $\square = \div$ and $\triangle = +$

   (B) $\square = +$ and $\triangle = \times$

   (C) $\square = \times$ and $\triangle = -$

   (D) $\square = -$ and $\triangle = \div$

14. How many square feet is equal to 1 square yard? (1 yard = 3 feet)

   (J)   3 ft^2

   (K)   6 ft^2

   (L)   9 ft^2

   (M) 12 ft^2

15. If the price of a cup is \$5. If the price is increased by 200%, what is the new price of the cup?

   (A) \$10

   (B) \$15

   (C) \$20

   (D) \$25

STOP

IAAT PRACTICE TEST 5

SECTION 2
Time — 10 minutes
15 Questions

Directions: Read the information given and choose the best answer for each question. Base your answer only on the information given. The time limit for each section is 10 minutes.

Directions: Use the table to answer questions 1 – 4.

Number of words in 1 page	60
Number of words Joshua type in 1 minute	30
Number of hours Joshua type in 1 day	2
Number of days Joshua type in 1 week	3

1. How long will take for Joshua to type 1 page?

   (A)   5 minutes

   (B)   4 minutes

   (C)   3 minutes

   (D)   2 minutes

2. How many hours will Joshua type in 1 week?

   (J)   6 hours

   (K)   7 hours

   (L)   8 hours

   (M)   10 hours

3. How many words can Joshua type in 1 day?

   (A)   3600 words

   (B)   4000 words

   (C)   4400 words

   (D)   4800 words

4. How many week does Joshua need to type 21600 words?

   (J)   6 weeks

   (K)   4 weeks

   (L)   3 weeks

   (M)   2 weeks

Directions: 200 people surveyed about their favorite color. The number of people people chose White as their favorite color is 15 more than the number of people chose Yellow as their favorite color. Use the table to answer questions 5 – 8.

Color	Pink	White	Yellow	Green	Blue
Number of people	20	50	35	55	40

5. How many people chose White as their favorite color?

   (A) 45

   (B) 50

   (C) 55

   (D) 60

7. What percentage of the people who surveyed chose Blue as their favorite?

   (A) 15%

   (B) 20%

   (C) 25%

   (D) 30%

6. How many people chose Green as their favorite color?

   (J) 50

   (K) 55

   (L) 60

   (M) 65

8. If one person is randomly selected, what is the probability that the person choose Green as his or her favorite color based on the survey?

   (J) 22.5%

   (K) 25%

   (L) 27.5%

   (M) 30%

9. Which of the following scatter plots contain data with NO relationship?

(A)

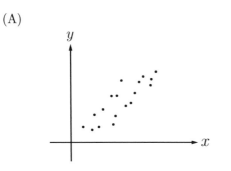

(B)

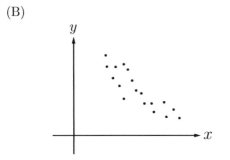

(C)

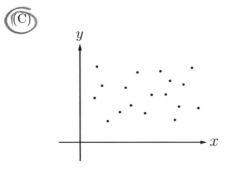

(D)

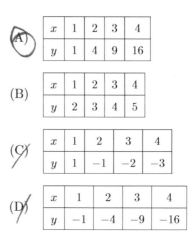

Directions: Use the graph to answer questions 10 – 11.

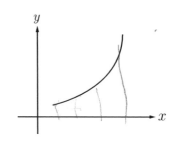

10. Which of the following phrase best represents the graph?

(J)   As x increases, y increases at a constant rate.

(K)   As x increases, y decreases at a constant rate.

(L)   As x increases, y increases rapidly.

(M)   As x increases, y decreases rapidly.

11. Which of the following table of ordered pairs is used to graph shown above?

(A)

x	1	2	3	4
y	1	4	9	16

(B)

x	1	2	3	4
y	2	3	4	5

(C)

x	1	2	3	4
y	1	-1	-2	-3

(D)

x	1	2	3	4
y	-1	-4	-9	-16

Directions: Use the data set to answer questions 12 − 15.

$$\{4, 5, 2, 9, 12, 7, 9, 10\}$$

12. What is the average of the data set?

    (J) 8

    (K) 7.75

    (L) 7.5

    (M) 7.25

13. What is the median of the data set?

    (A) 6

    (B) 7

    (C) 8

    (D) 9

14. What is the mode of the data set?

    (J) 12

    (K) 9

    (L) 7

    (M) 5

15. What is the range of the data set?

    (A) 13

    (B) 12

    (C) 11

    (D) 10

STOP

IAAT PRACTICE TEST 5

SECTION 3
Time — 10 minutes
15 Questions

Directions: Read the information given and choose the best answer for each question. Base your answer only on the information given. The time limit for each section is 10 minutes.

1. The density D is given by $D = \dfrac{M}{V}$ where M is the mass and V is the volume. What is the volume V in terms of the density D and the mass M ?

   (A) $V = D + M$

   (B) $V = DM$

   (C) $V = \dfrac{M}{D}$

   (D) $V = \dfrac{D}{M}$

2. Which of the following equation best represents the following verbal phrase? The number of cakes sold, x, is 20% less than the number of cups of coffee sold, y.

   (J) $y = 1.2x$

   (K) $y = 0.8x$

   (L) $x = 1.2y$

   (M) $x = 0.8y$

3. If $y = 2^x$, what is the value of y when $x = 3$?

   (A)   12

   (B)   9

   (C)   8

   (D)   6

4. Which of the following table of ordered pairs is used to graph a vertical line?

   (J)

x	2	2	2	2
y	-2	-1	1	2

   (K)

x	1	2	3	4
y	2	2	2	2

   (L)

x	1	2	3	4
y	1	2	3	4

   (M)

x	1	2	3	4
y	4	3	2	1

www.solomonacademy.net

$J, K, L, M, J, K, \cdots$

5. If the pattern continues, which letter is the 28th term?

(A) J

(B) K

(C) L

(D) M

6. The amount of a radioactive substance decreases by half every 13 seconds. How long does it take for the amount of the substance to decrease to one-eighth of the initial amount?

(J)   26 seconds

(K)   39 seconds

(L)   52 seconds

(M)   104 seconds

$\frac{1}{2}$

$\frac{1}{4}$

$1/8$

x	y
-1	8
0	6
2	2
3	0

7. A line passes through four ordered pairs in the table above. What is the y-intercept of the line?

(A) 8

(B) 6

(C) 4

(D) 3

The square of a number, n, decreased by 10 is 6.

8. Which of the following dquation represents the verbal phrase above?

(J) $n^2 - 10 = 6$

(K) $n^2 + 6 = 10$

(L) $2n - 10 = 6$

(M) $2n + 6 = 10$

$n^2 - 10 = 6$

9. If $\frac{x}{2} = \frac{8}{y}$, what is the product of x and y ?

$\frac{x}{2} = \frac{8}{y}$

(A) 2

(B) 6

(C) 8

(D) 16

x	100	49	16	4
y	10	7	4	2

10. The table shows four pairs of x and y values. Which is true for all values in the table shown above?

    (J) $y = \dfrac{x}{10}$

    (K) $y = 10x$

    (L) $y = x^2$

    (M) $y = \sqrt{x}$

11. The line $y = 10 - \dfrac{2}{3}x$ passes through the following ordered pairs EXCEPT

    (A) $(3, 9)$

    (B) $(6, 6)$

    (C) $(9, 4)$

    (D) $(12, 2)$

12. Albert Einstein's theory of special relativity states that the energy, E, is the mass of an object, M, times the speed of light, C, squared. Which of the following equation best represents Albert Einstein's theory of special relativity?

    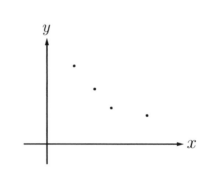

    (J) $\dfrac{E}{M} = C$

    (K) $E \times M = C$

    (L) $E = MC^2$

    (M) $E = (MC)^2$

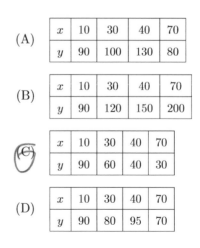

13. Which of the following table best represents the scatter plot?

    (A)

x	10	30	40	70
y	90	100	130	80

    (B)

x	10	30	40	70
y	90	120	150	200

    (C)

x	10	30	40	70
y	90	60	40	30

    (D)

x	10	30	40	70
y	90	80	95	70

14. At a grocery store, a customer purchased two bananas and four apples for $6.29. How much would the customer pay if he or she purchase four bananas and eight apples?

   (J) $25.16

   (K) $18.87

   (L) $12.58

   (M) $9.15

	Phone	Computer	TV	Stereo
Price	$399	$899	$999	$569
Unit Cost	$155	$561	$736	$324

15. The table above shows four items that an electronic store are selling. Profit of an item is defined by the price of an item minus unit cost of an item. Which of the following item gives the store greatest profit?

   (A)   Phone

   (B)   Computer

   (C)   TV

   (D)   Stereo

STOP

IAAT PRACTICE TEST 5

SECTION 4
Time — 10 minutes

15 Questions

Directions: Read the information given and choose the best answer for each question. Base your answer only on the information given. The time limit for each section is 10 minutes.

1. 5 years ago, Jason was x years old. How old will he be in 5 years from now?

   (A) x

   (B) $x + 10$

   (C) $2x + 5$

   (D) $5x$

2. Which of the following value of x satisfies the equation $2(x + 1) + 1 = 3$?

   (J) 3

   (K) 2

   (L) 1

   (M) 0

3. Which of the following value of x satisfies the inequality $-\dfrac{x}{2} < -4$?

   (A) $x > 8$

   (B) $x < 8$

   (C) $x > -8$

   (D) $x < -8$

4. Simplify the expression: $x^2 - 2x^2 + 3x^2$

   (J) $-6x^2$

   (K) $2x^2$

   (L) $4x^2$

   (M) $6x^2$

5. $a \circledR b$ gives you a remainder when a is divided by b. What is $62 \circledR 7$?

   (A) 1

   (B) 4

   (C) 5

   (D) 6

6. Joshua has n quarters and k nickels. How much money, in cents, does Joshua have in terms of n and k ?

   (J) 30

   (K) $30 + n + k$

   (L) $25n + 5k$

   (M) $30(n + k)$

7. The price of a jacket is P, and the sales tax rate is 5%. If Mr. Rhee pays \$300 including the sales tax when he buys the jacket, which equation should be used to calculate the price of the jacket P?

(A) $1.05P = 300$

(B) $1.5P = 300$

(C) $\dfrac{P}{0.05} = 300$

(D) $\dfrac{P}{1.05} = 300$

The mean of x and y minus 3.

8. How is the following verbal phrase above expressed algebraically?

(J) $3 - (x + y)$

(K) $x + y - 3$

(L) $3 - \dfrac{x + y}{2}$

(M) $\dfrac{x + y}{2} - 3$

9. If $6^2 + x^2 = 100$, what could be value of x ?

(A) -6

(B) -7

(C) -8

(D) -9

10. If $y + 2x = 20 - y$, what is the sum of x and y ?

(J) 5

(K) 10

(L) 15

(M) 20

The sum of two consecutive integers is 21.

11. Which of the following equation best represents the verbal phrase above ? (Assuming the smaller is x)

(A) $x \cdot x = 21$

(B) $x(x + 1) = 21$

(C) $x + (x + 1) = 21$

(D) $x + 2x = 21$

12. Which of the following value of x satisfies the equation $|x - 1| = 2$?

(J) -1

(K) 1

(L) 2

(M) 4

13. If the length of a cube is $2x$, what is the surface area of the cube?

(A) $6x^2$

(B) $12x^2$

(C) $18x^2$

(D) $24x^2$

14. 1 hour has 60 minutes and 1 minute has 60 seconds. How many seconds are there in t hours?

(J) $60t$

(K) $120t$

(L) $600t$

(M) $3600t$

15. Joshua wants to save \$$n$ to buy a tablet computer. If he saves \$$k$ every week, which expression best represents how many weeks he needs to save to buy the tablet computer?

(A) $\dfrac{k}{n}$

(B) $\dfrac{n}{k}$

(C) nk

(D) $n + k$

Answers and Solutions

IAAT Practice Test 5 Section 1

Answers

1. B	2. L	3. A	4. L	5. B
6. K	7. D	8. J	9. C	10. M
11. B	12. K	13. C	14. L	15. B

Solutions

1. (B)

   The dimension of a matrix is the number of rows by the number of columns of the matrix. Since the matrix has two rows and three columns, the dimension of the matrix is 2 by 3. Therefore, (B) is the correct answer.

2. (L)

$$1 \text{ ton } = 2000 \text{ pounds} \qquad \text{Multiply both sides by 1.5}$$
$$1.5 \text{ ton } = 1.5 \times 2000 \text{ pounds}$$
$$1.5 \text{ ton } = 3000 \text{ pounds}$$

   Therefore, (L) is the correct answer.

3. (A)

   $1.24 + 0.86 + 2.1 = 4.2$. Therefore, (A) is the correct answer.

4. (L)

   A quarter is worth 25 cents, a dime is worth 10 cents, and a nickel is worth 5 cents. Since there are seven quarters, three dimes, and two nickels in the coin purse, the total amount of money in the coin purse is $7 \times 25 + 3 \times 10 + 2 \times 5 = 215$ cents or \$2.15. Therefore, (L) is the correct answer.

5. (B)

   A prime number has only two factors: 1 and itself. 8 is not a prime number so that it has more than two factors. Therefore, (B) is the correct answer.

6. (K)

   The average of the five numbers is the sum of five numbers divided by 5. The sum of the five numbers is $240 + 10 = 250$. Thus, the average of the five numbers is $\frac{250}{5} = 50$. Therefore, (K) is the correct answer.

7. (D)

$$1 \text{ hour} = 60 \text{ minutes} \qquad \text{Multiply both sides by } 5.4$$
$$5.4 \text{ hour} = 5.4 \times 60 \text{ minutes}$$
$$5.4 \text{ hour} = 324 \text{ minutes}$$

Therefore, (D) is the correct answer.

8. (J)

$\dfrac{25}{3} \div \dfrac{3}{4} = \dfrac{25}{3} \times \dfrac{4}{3} = \dfrac{100}{9}$. Therefore, (J) is the correct answer.

9. (C)

Joshua walks due West at a rate of 3 ft/s. Jason walks due East at a rate of 2 ft/s. Since they walk in opposite direction, they are apart $3 + 2$ or 5 feet every second. Thus, they are apart 5×7 feet or 35 feet in 7 seconds. Therefore, (C) is the correct answer.

10. (M)

$8\pi = 8 \times 3.14 = 25.12$. Therefore, (M) is the correct answer.

11. (B)

$\dfrac{2}{5} = 0.4 = 40\%$. Therefore, (B) is the correct answer.

12. (K)

$$8 \times 10^2 \times 5 \times 10^3 = 8 \times 5 \times 10^2 \times 10^3$$
$$= 40 \times 10^5$$
$$= 4 \times 10 \times 10^5$$
$$= 4 \times 10^6$$

Therefore, (K) is the correct answer.

13. (C)

Since $4 \times 3 - 2 = 10$, $\square = \times$, and $\triangle = -$. Therefore, (C) is the correct answer.

14. (L)

$$1 \text{ yd}^2 = 1 \text{ yard} \times 1 \text{ yard}$$
$$= 3 \text{ ft} \times 3 \text{ ft}$$
$$= 9 \text{ ft}^2$$

15. (B)

$200\% = 2$. The price of a cup is \$5. Since the price of the cup is increased by 200%, the new price of the cup is $5 + 200\%(5)$ or $5 + 2(5) = 15$. Therefore, (B) is the correct answer.

Answers and Solutions

IAAT Practice Test 5 Section 2

Answers

1. D	2. J	3. A	4. M	5. B
6. K	7. B	8. L	9. C	10. L
11. A	12. M	13. C	14. K	15. D

Solutions

1. (D)

According to the table, Joshua types 30 words in 1 minute. Since there are 60 words in 1 page, it takes for Joshua to type 60 words in 2 minutes. Therefore, (D) is the correct answer.

2. (J)

Joshua types 2 hours in 1 day and 3 days in 1 week. Thus, he types 2×3 or 6 hours in 1 week. Therefore, (J) is the correct answer.

3. (A)

Joshua types 30 words in a minute. There are 60 minutes in 1 hour. So, Joshua can type 30×60 or 1800 words in 1 hour. Since Joshua types 2 hours in a day, he can type 1800×2 or 3600 words in a day. Therefore, (A) is the correct answer.

4. (M)

Joshua types 3 days in a week. He can type 3600 words in a day. So, Joshua can type 3×3600 or 10800 words in a week. Therefore, it will take for Joshua to type 21600 words in 2 weeks. Therefore, (M) is the correct answer.

5. (B)

The number of White is 15 more than the number of Yellow. So, the number of White is $35 + 15 = 50$. Therefore, (B) is the correct answer.

6. (K)

The number of Green is $200 - (20 + 50 + 35 + 40) = 55$. Therefore, (K) is the correct answer.

7. (B)

The percentage of the people who surveyed chose Blue as their favorite is $\frac{40}{200} = 0.2 = 20\%$. Therefore, (B) is the correct answer.

8. (L)

The probability that the person choose Green as his or her favorite color based on the survey is $\frac{55}{200} = 0.275 = 27.5\%$. Therefore, (L) is the correct answer.

9. (C)

A scatter plot with no relationship shows that y does not increase nor decrease as x increases. Therefore, (C) is the correct answer.

10. (L)

The graph represents that y increases more than 1 as x increases by 1. Therefore, (L) is the correct answer.

11. (A)

The table contains a list of ordered pairs: $(1, 1)$, $(2, 4)$, $(3, 9)$, and $(4, 16)$. If you plot these ordered pairs in the xy-coordinate plane, the graph will be similar to the graph shown in problem 10. Therefore, (A) is the correct answer.

12. (M)

$$\text{Average} = \frac{4 + 5 + 2 + 9 + 12 + 7 + 9 + 10}{8} = 7.25$$

Therefore, (M) is the correct answer.

13. (C)

Arrange the numbers from least to greatest: $\{2, 4, 5, 7, 9, 9, 10, 12\}$. Since there are 8 numbers in the data set, the median is the average of the fourth and fifth numbers; that is, $\frac{7 + 9}{2} = 8$. Therefore, (C) is the correct answer.

14. (K)

The mode is a number that is most shown frequently. Since there are two 9 in the data set, 9 is the mode. Therefore, (K) is the correct answer.

15. (D)

The range of the data set is the difference of the greatest number and least number in the data set. Since 12 is the greatest number and 2 is the least number, the range of the data set is $12 - 2 = 10$. Therefore, (D) is the correct answer.

Answers and Solutions
IAAT Practice Test 5 Section 3

Answers

1. C	2. M	3. C	4. J	5. D
6. K	7. B	8. J	9. D	10. M
11. A	12. L	13. C	14. L	15. B

Solutions

1. (C)

$$D = \frac{M}{V} \qquad \text{Multiply both sides by } V$$
$$DV = M \qquad \text{Divide both sides by } D$$
$$V = \frac{M}{D}$$

Therefore, (C) is the correct answer.

2. (M)

x is 20% less than y means that x is 80% of y, which can be written as $x = 0.8y$. Therefore, (M) is the correct answer.

3. (C)

When $x = 3$, $y = 2^3 = 2 \times 2 \times 2 = 8$. Therefore, (C) is the correct answer.

4. (J)

The table in (J) contains a set of ordered pairs: $(2, -2)$, $(2, -1)$, $(2, 1)$, and $(2, 2)$. Connecting these ordered pairs will give a vertical line. Therefore, (J) is the correct answer.

5. (D)

J, K, L, M is a pattern from which every fourth letter is M. In other words, 4th, 8th, 12th, $\cdots$, 28th letters are M. Therefore, (D) is the correct answer.

6. (K)

Let A be the initial amount of the radioactive substance. Since the amount of a radioactive substance decreases by half every 13 seconds,

Time (seconds)	0	13	26	39
Amount	A	$\frac{A}{2}$	$\frac{A}{4}$	$\frac{A}{8}$

the amount of the radioactive substance is one-eighth of the initial amount after 39 seconds. Therefore, (K) is the correct answer.

7. (B)

The y-intercept is an ordered pair on the y-axis. Since the table contains an ordered pair $(0,6)$ which is on the y-axis, (B) is the correct answer.

8. (J)

The square of a number, n, decreased by 10 is 6 can be written as $n^2 - 10 = 6$. Therefore, (J) is the correct answer.

9. (D)

Cross multiply $\frac{x}{2} = \frac{8}{y}$ gives $xy = 16$, which means that the product of x and y is 16. Therefore, (D) is the correct answer.

10. (M)

Since $10 = \sqrt{100}$, and $7 = \sqrt{49}$, $y = \sqrt{x}$. Therefore, (M) is the correct answer.

11. (A)

Substituting 3 for x in $y = 10 - \frac{2}{3}x$ gives

$$y = 10 - \frac{2}{3}(3) = 8$$

$y = 8$. Thus, an ordered pair $(3, 8)$ is on the line, not $(3, 9)$. Therefore, (A) is the correct answer.

12. (L)

The special relativity which states that the energy, E, is the mass of an object, M, times the speed of light, C, squared can be expressed as $E = MC^2$.

13. (C)

The scatter plot shows that y decreases as x increases. Since the table in (C) best represents the relationship between x and y, (C) is the correct answer.

14. (L)

If a customer wants to buy twice as many as bananas and apples before, he or she would pay twice as much as before, which is $2 \times \$6.29 = \$12.58$. Therefore, (L) is the correct answer.

15. (B)

According to the table that shows the profit of the four items,

Items	Profit = Price − Unit Cost
Phone	$399 - 155 = 244$
Computer	$899 - 561 = 338$
TV	$999 - 736 = 263$
Stereo	$569 - 324 = 245$

computer gives the store greatest profit. Therefore, (B) is the correct answer.

Answers and Solutions
IAAT Practice Test 5 Section 4

Answers

1. B	2. M	3. A	4. K	5. D
6. L	7. A	8. M	9. C	10. K
11. C	12. J	13. D	14. M	15. B

Solutions

1. (B)

   Jason was x years old 5 years ago, which means that he is $x + 5$ years old now. In 5 years, he will be $x + 5 + 5$ or $x + 10$ years old. Therefore, (B) is the correct answer.

2. (M)

$$2(x + 1) + 1 = 3 \qquad \text{Use the distributive property: } a(b + c) = ab + ac$$
$$2x + 2 + 1 = 3$$
$$2x + 3 = 3$$
$$2x = 0$$
$$x = 0$$

   Therefore, (M) is the correct answer.

3. (A)

$$-\frac{x}{2} < -4 \qquad \text{Multiply both sides by } -2$$
$$x > 8 \qquad \text{Reverse the inequality symbol when you multiply a negative number}$$

   Therefore, (A) is the correct answer.

4. (K)

   $x^2 - 2x^2 + 3x^2 = 2x^2$. Therefore, (K) is the correct answer.

5. (D)

   $a \circledR b$ gives you a remainder when a is divided by b. When 62 is divided by 7, the quotient is 8, and the remainder is 6. Thus, $62 \circledR 7 = 6$. Therefore, (D) is the correct answer.

6. (L)

   A quarter is worth 25 cents and a nickel is worth 5 cents. If Joshua has n quarters and k nickels, the amount of money that Joshua has, in cents, is $25n + 5k$. Therefore, (L) is the correct answer.

7. (A)

The price of a jacket is P, and the sales tax rate is 5%. Thus, the tax is $5\% \times P = 0.05P$. Since Mr. Rhee pays $300 which includes the price of the jacket and the tax, $P + 0.05P = 300$, or $1.05P = 300$. Therefore, (A) is the correct answer.

8. (M)

The mean or average of x and y is $\dfrac{x+y}{2}$. Thus, the mean of x and y minus 3 is $\dfrac{x+y}{2} - 3$. Therefore, (M) is the correct answer.

9. (C)

$$6^2 + x^2 = 100$$
$$x^2 = 64$$
$$x = 8 \quad \text{or} \quad x = -8$$

Therefore, (C) is the correct answer.

10. (K)

$$y + 2x = 20 - y \qquad \text{Add } y \text{ to both sides}$$
$$2x + 2y = 20 \qquad \text{Divide both sides by 2}$$
$$x + y = 10$$

Thus, the sum of x and y is $x + y = 10$. Therefore, (K) is the correct answer.

11. (C)

Consecutive integers are integers that follow each other in order. They have a difference of 1 between every two numbers. If the smaller integer is x, then the larger integer is $x+1$. Thus, the sum of two consecutive integers is 21 can be expressed as $x + (x+1) = 21$. Therefore, (C) is the correct answer.

12. (J)

Substituting -1 for x in $|x - 1| = 2$ gives $|-2| = 2$, which is true. Thus, $x = -1$ satisfies the equation $|x - 1| = 2$. Therefore, (J) is the correct answer.

13. (D)

Each side of a cube is a square. The area A of each face of a cube with side length $2x$ is $A = (2x)^2 = 4x^2$. Since there are 6 faces, the surface area of the cube is $6 \times 4x^2 = 24x^2$. Therefore, (D) is the correct answer.

14. (M)

1 hour has 60 minutes and 1 minute has 60 seconds, which means that there are 60×60 or 3600 seconds in 1 hour. Thus, there are $3600 \times t$ or $3600t$ seconds in t hours. Therefore, (M) is the correct answer.

15. (B)

Joshua saves $$k$ every week. Let x be the number of weeks that Joshua needs to save. In x weeks, he will save $$xk$, which is equal to n. Thus,

$$xk = n \qquad \text{Divide both sides by } k$$
$$x = \frac{n}{k}$$

Thus, the number of weeks that Joshua needs to save to buy the tablet computer is $\frac{n}{k}$. Therefore, (B) is the correct answer.

IAAT PRACTICE TEST 6

SECTION 1
Time — 10 minutes
15 Questions

Directions: Read the information given and choose the best answer for each question. Base your answer only on the information given. The time limit for each section is 10 minutes.

1. What is the greatest common factor (GCF) of 36 and 54?

    (A) 24

    (B) 18

    (C) 15

    (D) 12

2. The speed of light is $300,000,000$ m/s. Which of the following represents the speed of light in scientific notation?

    (J) 3×10^9 m/s

    (K) 3×10^8 m/s

    (L) 3×10^7 m/s

    (M) 3×10^6 m/s

3. $\begin{bmatrix} 7 & 3 \\ 1 & 2 \end{bmatrix} - \begin{bmatrix} 2 & 1 \\ -1 & 2 \end{bmatrix} =$

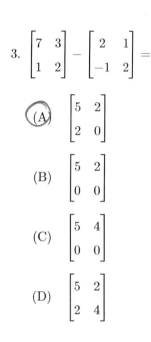

    (A) $\begin{bmatrix} 5 & 2 \\ 2 & 0 \end{bmatrix}$

    (B) $\begin{bmatrix} 5 & 2 \\ 0 & 0 \end{bmatrix}$

    (C) $\begin{bmatrix} 5 & 4 \\ 0 & 0 \end{bmatrix}$

    (D) $\begin{bmatrix} 5 & 2 \\ 2 & 4 \end{bmatrix}$

4. Jason has a map that uses a scale of $\frac{1}{2}$ inch for every 5 miles. If Joshua draws a 3 inch-long line on the map for his bicycle path, which of the following best represents actual distance, in miles, of his bicycle path?

    (J) 15

    (K) 20

    (L) 25

    (M) 30

5. Evaluate: $\frac{11}{3} - 2\frac{1}{3}$

   (A) $2\frac{2}{3}$

   (B) $2\frac{1}{3}$

   (C) $1\frac{2}{3}$

   (D) $1\frac{1}{3}$

6. Every \$100 you earn, income tax is \$8. If Sue earns \$5000, how much does she pay for income tax?

   (J)   \$500

   (K)   \$480

   (L)   \$400

   (M)   \$360

7. Evaluate: $2 + 3 \times 3^2 - 1$

   (A)   44

   (B)   35

   (C)   28

   (D)   26

8. $1.4 \times 10^{-3} =$

   (J)   0.00014

   (K)   0.0014

   (L)   140

   (M)   1400

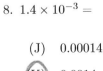

9. Which of the following is an irrational number?

   (A) $\frac{7}{8}$

   (B)   0.3

   (C) $\sqrt{2}$

   (D)   3

10. There are 30 students in a class. 20% of the students play football, 50% of the students play baseball, and the remaining students do not play any sport. How many students do NOT play any sport in the class?

   (J)   9

   (K)   10

   (L)   12

   (M)   15

11. Which of the following statement is true?

   (A) $\frac{2}{5} > 0.35$

   (B) $75\% < \frac{2}{3}$

   (C) $0.12 > 1 \times 10^2$

   (D) $3 > \sqrt{16}$

www.solomonacademy.net

$$\Box - 13 - 26 = 57$$

12. What number goes to the box shown above so that the equation is true?

(J) 96

(K) 98

(L) 100

(M) 102

13. 2000 pounds is equal to 1 ton. How many pounds is equal to 0.3 ton?

(A) 900 pounds

(B) 800 pounds

(C) 700 pounds

(D) 600 pounds

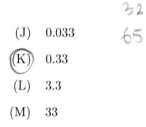

14. Joshua has 2 quarters and 3 nickels, and Jason has 3 dimes and 2 pennies. How much more money, in dollar, does Joshua have than Jason?

(J) 0.033

(K) 0.33

(L) 3.3

(M) 33

15. A ball is dropped from 100 ft. Each time it hits the ground, it rebounds to one-half its previous height. How many feet will it rebound after it hits the ground for the third time?

(A) 25 feet

(B) 18 feet

(C) 12.5 feet

(D) 6.25 feet

STOP

IAAT PRACTICE TEST 6

SECTION 2
Time — 10 minutes
15 Questions

Directions: Read the information given and choose the best answer for each question. Base your answer only on the information given. The time limit for each section is 10 minutes.

Directions: Train A and train B left the same station at 12 PM. The graph below shows the speed of the two trains over time. Use the graph to answer questions 1 − 4.

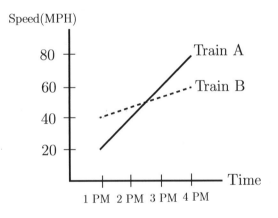

1. What is the speed of train A at 1 PM?

(A)   60 MPH

(B)   40 MPH

(C)   20 MPH

(D)   10 MPH

2. What is the speed of train B at 4 PM?

(J)   30 MPH

(K)   40 MPH

(L)   50 MPH

(M)   60 MPH

3. From which time period does train B travel faster than train A?

(A)   1 PM to 4 PM

(B)   3 PM to 4 PM

(C)   2 PM to 3 PM

(D)   1 PM to 2 PM

4. At what time do both trains travel at the same speed?

(J)   2:30 PM

(K)   3:00 PM

(L)   3:30 PM

(M)   4:00 PM

Directions: Use the following graph to answer questions 5 − 8.

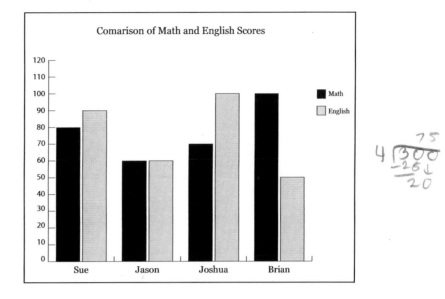

5. Who has the highest Math score?

   (A) Sue

   (B) Jason

   (C) Joshua

   (D) Brian

6. Whose English score is 10 more than his or her Math score?

   (J) Sue

   (K) Jason

   (L) Joshua

   (M) Brian

7. What is the average of English scores among four students?

   (A) 75

   (B) 80

   (C) 85

   (D) 90

8. How many students receive higher English score than Math score?

   (J) 1

   (K) 2

   (L) 3

   (M) 4

Directions: Use the graph to answer questions 9 – 12.

Survey of Favorite Fruits

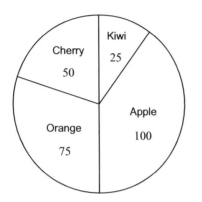

9. What is the total number of people surveyed?

 (A) 200

 (B) 250

 (C) 300

 (D) 350

10. What percent of those surveyed favored kiwi?

 (J) 5%

 (K) 10%

 (L) 15%

 (M) 20%

11. What percent of those surveyed favored either orange or cherry?

 (A) 50%

 (B) 55%

 (C) 60%

 (D) 65%

12. According to the pie chart, what is the probability that a person chosen at random selects an apple as his or her favorite fruit?

 (J) $\dfrac{3}{4}$

 (K) $\dfrac{3}{5}$

 (L) $\dfrac{1}{2}$

 (M) $\dfrac{2}{5}$

Directions: Jason surveyed all students in his class about after school activities. They are taking either tennis or football. There are 15 students are taking tennis, 25 students are taking football, and 5 students are taking both tennis and football. Use the following venn diagram to answer questions 13 − 15.

After school Activities

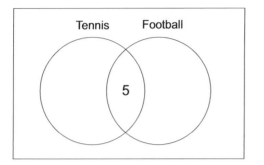

13. How many students are taking only tennis?

    (A)   25

    (B)   20

    (C)   15

    (D)   10

14. How many students are taking only football?

    (J)   30

    (K)   25

    (L)   20

    (M)   15

15. What is the total number of students in Jason's class?

    (A)   45

    (B)   40

    (C)   35

    (D)   30

IAAT PRACTICE TEST 6

SECTION 3
Time — 10 minutes
15 Questions

Directions: Read the information given and choose the best answer for each question. Base your answer only on the information given. The time limit for each section is 10 minutes.

1. Which of the following is a function?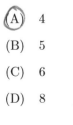

   (A) $\{(1,4), (2,5), (3,3), (4,2)\}$

   (B) $\{(1,3), (3,1), (5,4), (1,2)\}$

   (C) $\{(1,2), (2,4), (2,-1), (3,-1)\}$

   (D) $\{(1,4), (2,2), (3,9), (3,3)\}$

2. Which of the following equation has an undefined slope?

   (J) $y = x + 3$

   (K) $y = 1$

   (L) $x = 1$

   (M) $y = -x - 2$

3. If $x = 2$ and $y = 8$, what is the value of $\sqrt{xy}$?

   (A) 4

   (B) 5

   (C) 6

   (D) 8

Length (L)	Price (P)
10	100
20	400
30	900
40	1600

4. The table above shows the length, L, and price, P, of a certain material. Which of the following equation best represents the relationship between the length and price of the material?

   (J) $P = L + 10$

   (K) $P = L + 90$

   (L) $P = 2L$

   (M) $P = L^2$

5. Which of the following equation best represents the following verbal relationship? The number of oranges, O, is 20 more than twice the number of apples, A.

   (A) $O = A + 20$

   (B) $O = 2A - 20$

   (C) $O = 2A + 20$

   (D) $O = 40A$

6. The product of x and y is 20. Which of the following tables represent this relationship?

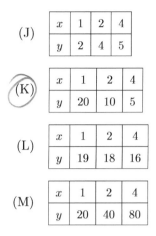

(J)

x	1	2	4
y	2	4	5

(K)

x	1	2	4
y	20	10	5

(L)

x	1	2	4
y	19	18	16

(M)

x	1	2	4
y	20	40	80

Input	Output
2	
6	4
10	6
14	8

7. Observe the numbers in the two columns in order to determine which of the following value should be in the empty cell.

(A)　6

(B)　4

(C)　3

(D)　2

$$\frac{2}{3}(12 - 6)$$

8. Which of the following expression is equivalent to the expression shown above?

(J)　$\frac{2}{3} \times 12 - \frac{2}{3} \times 6$

(K)　$\frac{2}{3} \times 12 - \frac{2}{3} \times 1$

(L)　$\frac{2}{3} \times 12 + \frac{2}{3} \times 6$

(M)　$\frac{2}{3} \times 12 + \frac{2}{3} \times 1$

9. Which of the following ordered pair does the line $y = -x$ passes through?

(A)　$(-2, -2)$

(B)　$(-1, 1)$

(C)　$(0, -1)$

(D)　$(1, 1)$

10. Which of the following equation of line has the steepest slope?

(J)　$y = 3x - 2$

(K)　$y = 5x + 3$

(L)　$y = -x + 2$

(M)　$y = -2x + 5$

11. Which equation best represents the following situation? The cost of renting a bus is $k. If the cost is equally distributed among 10 students, how much does each person pay?

   (A) $(k + 10)$

   (B) $10k$

   (C) $(k - 10)$

   (D) $\dfrac{k}{10}$

12. A yard is equal to 36 inches. Which of the following equation best converts X yards to Y inches?

   (J) $X = Y + 36$

   (K) $X = 36Y$

   (L) $Y = 36X$

   (M) $Y = X + 36$

13. Which of the following table best represents the following verbal relationship? The price of a shirt, y, is 25% of the price of a jacket, x.

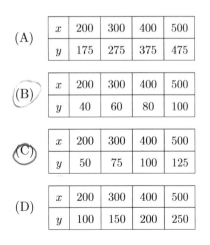

(A)

x	200	300	400	500
y	175	275	375	475

(B)

x	200	300	400	500
y	40	60	80	100

(C)

x	200	300	400	500
y	50	75	100	125

(D)

x	200	300	400	500
y	100	150	200	250

x	6	8	10
y	0	-2	-4

14. The table above contains ordered pairs that are solutions to which of the following equation?

   (J) $y = x - 6$

   (K) $y = x + 6$

   (L) $y = -x + 6$

   (M) $y = -x - 6$

$$\{(-1, 5),\ (0, 2),\ (1, -1),\ (2, -4)\}$$

15. Which equation represents the relationship of the set of ordered pairs shown above?

   (A) $y = -x + 4$

   (B) $y = -2x - 3$

   (C) $y = -3x + 2$

   (D) $y = -5x$

STOP

IAAT PRACTICE TEST 6

SECTION 4
Time — 10 minutes
15 Questions

Directions: Read the information given and choose the best answer for each question. Base your answer only on the information given. The time limit for each section is 10 minutes.

1. Solve for x: $\dfrac{x}{5} = \dfrac{3}{5}$

   (A)   2

   (B)   3

   (C)   4

   (D)   5

2. $-x(x + y) =$

   (J) $-2x + xy$

   (K) $-2x - xy$

   (L) $x^2 - x + y$

   (M) $-x^2 - xy$

3. If $x = 2$ and $y = -3$, which of the following expression has the smallest value?

   (A) $x - y$

   (B) $-x + y$

   (C) $-xy$

   (D) $2xy$

4. If $2x - y - 7 = 0$, what is the value of $2x - y$?

   (J) -7

   (K) -3

   (L) 3

   (M) 7

5. If $a \spadesuit b = \dfrac{b - a}{a + b}$, what is the value of $-2 \spadesuit 4$?

   (A) 3

   (B) 2

   (C) -2

   (D) -3

6. Which of the following value satisfies the inequality $-x + 3 < 2$?

   (J) 2

   (K) 1

   (L) 0

   (M) -1

7. Jason can wash n cars in 2 hours. How many cars can he wash in 6 hours?

(A) $n + 4$

(B) $2n$

(C) $3n$

(D) $4n + 4$

8. The volume of a cone is defined as $V = \frac{1}{3}\pi r^2 h$, where r and h are the radius and height, respectively. What is the volume of a cone that has a height of 9 and a radius of 2?

(J) 2π

(K) 6π

(L) 12π

(M) 16π

9. Simplify the expression $2x + y - z + y$.

(A) $2x - z$

(B) $2x - 2y$

(C) $2y - z$

(D) $2z - 2y$

10. Which of the following inequality is true?

(J) $0 \geq -2$

(K) $0 > 0$

(L) $0 \leq -1$

(M) $0 < -1$

11. The formula for the surface area, A, of a cube is $A = 6x^2$, where x is the length of the cube. What is the surface area of a cube if the length of the cube is 6?

(A) 36

(B) 72

(C) 152

(D) 216

$$2\,(\,4\,\square\,3\,) = 14$$

12. Which of the following can be placed in the box to make the equation true?

(J) $\times$

(K) $\div$

(L) $+$

(M) $-$

13. which phrase is represented by $\frac{4}{x} + 1$?

(A) The product of four and a number, x, less one.

(B) One more than the quotient of four and a number, x.

(C) One more than the sum of four and a number, x.

(D) The quotient of four and a number, x, less one.

14. The perimeter of a square is 16. If each side of the square is increased by 2, what is the perimeter of new square?

(J) 18

(K) 20

(L) 22

(M) 24

15. Let $e(x)$ be the sum of all even numbers less than or equal to x. For instance, $e(6) = 2 + 4 + 6 = 12$. What is the value of $e(11)$?

(A) 26

(B) 30

(C) 34

(D) 38

STOP

Answers and Solutions
IAAT Practice Test 6 Section 1

Answers

1. B	2. K	3. A	4. M	5. D
6. L	7. C	8. K	9. C	10. J
11. A	12. J	13. D	14. K	15. C

Solutions

1. (B)

   Factors of 36 and 54 are as follows:

   $$36 = \{1, 2, 3, 4, 6, 9, 12, 18, 36\}$$
   $$54 = \{1, 2, 3, 6, 9, 18, 27, 54\}$$

   The greatest common factor (GCF) of 36 and 54 is 18. Therefore, (B) is the correct answer.

2. (K)

   The speed of light in scientific notation is $300,000,000 = 3 \times 100,000,000 = 3 \times 10^8$ m/s. Therefore, (K) is the correct answer.

3. (A)

   Subtraction of two matrices is done entry-wise.

   $$\begin{bmatrix} 7 & 3 \\ 1 & 2 \end{bmatrix} - \begin{bmatrix} 2 & 1 \\ -1 & 2 \end{bmatrix} = \begin{bmatrix} 7-2 & 3-1 \\ 1-(-1) & 2-2 \end{bmatrix} = \begin{bmatrix} 5 & 2 \\ 2 & 0 \end{bmatrix}$$

   Therefore, (A) is the correct answer.

4. (M)

   Set up a proportion: $\dfrac{\frac{1}{2}}{5} = \dfrac{3}{x}$. Cross multiply and solve for x. $\frac{1}{2}x = 15$ gives $x = 30$. Thus, 3 inch-long line on the map represents 30 miles. Therefore, (M) is the correct answer.

5. (D)

   $\dfrac{11}{3} - 2\dfrac{1}{3} = \dfrac{11}{3} - \dfrac{7}{3} = \dfrac{4}{3} = 1\dfrac{1}{3}$. Therefore, (D) is the correct answer.

6. (L)

Every $100 you earn, income tax is $8, which implies that the income tax rate is 8%. Thus, the income tax for $5000 is $5000 \times 0.08 = $400. Therefore, (L) is the correct answer.

7. (C)

$2 + 3 \times 3^2 - 1 = 2 + 3 \times 9 - 1 = 2 + 27 - 1 = 28$. Therefore, (C) is the correct answer.

8. (K)

Since $10^{-3} = \dfrac{1}{1000} = 0.001$, $1.4 \times 10^{-3} = 1.4 \times 0.001 = 0.0014$. Therefore, (K) is the correct answer.

9. (C)

Irrational numbers, when written as decimals, do not terminate, nor do they repeat. Since $\sqrt{2} = 1.4142135 \cdots$ does not terminate, it is an irrational number. Therefore, (C) is the correct answer.

10. (J)

$20\% + 50\% = 70\%$ students in the class play sports, which means that 30% of student in the class do not play any sports. The number of students in the class do not any sports is $30 \times 30\% = 30 \times 0.3 = 9$. Therefore, (J) is the correct answer.

11. (A)

$\dfrac{2}{5} = 0.4$. Thus, $\dfrac{2}{5} > 0.35$. Therefore, (A) is the correct answer.

12. (J)

$$\square - 13 - 26 = 57$$
$$\square = 57 + 13 + 26$$
$$\square = 96$$

Therefore, (J) is the correct answer.

13. (D)

$$1 \text{ ton} = 2000 \text{ pounds} \qquad \text{Multiply both sides by 0.3}$$
$$0.3 \text{ ton} = 0.3 \times 2000 \text{ pounds}$$
$$0.3 \text{ ton} = 600 \text{ pounds}$$

Therefore, (D) is the correct answer.

14. (K)

Joshua has 2 quarters and 3 nickels which means Joshua has 65 cents. Jason has 3 dimes and 2 pennies, which means Jason has 32 cents. Thus, Joshua has 33 cents or $0.33 more than Jason has. Therefore, (K) is the correct answer.

15. (C)

A ball is dropped from 100 ft. Each time it hits the ground, it rebounds to one-half its previous height. Thus,

First rebound	Height is 50 feet
Second rebound	Height is 25 feet
Third rebound	Height is 12.5 feet

Therefore, (C) is the correct answer.

Answers and Solutions
IAAT Practice Test 6 Section 2

Answers

1. C	2. M	3. D	4. J	5. D
6. J	7. A	8. K	9. B	10. K
11. A	12. M	13. D	14. L	15. C

Solutions

1. (C)

   The speed of train A at 1 PM is 20 MPH. Therefore, (C) is the correct answer.

2. (M)

   The speed of train B at 4 PM is 60 MPH. Therefore, (M) is the correct answer.

3. (D)

   Train B travels faster than train A between 1 PM to 2:30 PM. Therefore, (D) is the correct answer.

4. (J)

   At 2:30 PM, both trains travel at the same speed. Therefore, (J) is the correct answer.

5. (D)

   Brian received the highest Math score among four students. Therefore, (D) is the correct answer.

6. (J)

   Sue received 90 on English and 80 on Math. Therefore, (J) is the correct answer.

7. (A)

   The average of English scores among four students is $\dfrac{90 + 60 + 100 + 50}{4} = 75$. Therefore, (A) is the correct answer.

8. (K)

   Both Sue and Joshua received higher English score than Math score. Therefore, (K) is the correct answer.

9. (B)

   The total number of people surveyed is $25 + 100 + 75 + 50 = 250$. Therefore, (B) is the correct answer.

10. (K)

The percent of those surveyed favored kiwi is $\dfrac{25}{250} = \dfrac{1}{10} = 10\%$. Therefore, (K) is the correct answer.

11. (A)

The percent of those surveyed favored either orange or cherry is $\dfrac{75}{250} + \dfrac{50}{250} = \dfrac{125}{250} = 50\%$. Therefore, (A) is the correct answer.

12. (M)

The probability that a person chosen at random selects an apple as his or her favorite fruit is $\dfrac{100}{250} = \dfrac{2}{5}$. Therefore, (M) is the correct answer.

13. (D)

According to Figure 1, the number of students are taking only tennis is 10.

After school Activities

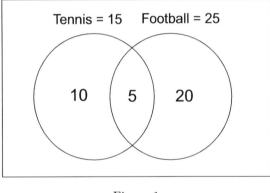

Figure 1

Therefore, (D) is the correct answer.

14. (L)

According to Figure 1 shown above, the number of students are taking only football is 20. Therefore, (L) is the correct answer.

15. (C)

The total number of students in Jason's class is $10 + 5 + 20 = 35$. Therefore, (C) is the correct answer.

Answers and Solutions

IAAT Practice Test 6 Section 3

Answers

1. A	2. L	3. A	4. M	5. C
6. K	7. D	8. J	9. B	10. K
11. D	12. L	13. C	14. L	15. C

Solutions

1. (A)

   The definition of a function is a set of ordered pairs whose x-values are not repeated. Since x values of ordered pairs in (A) are not repeated, (A) is the correct answer.

2. (L)

   The equation $x = 1$ represents a vertical line whose slope is undefined. Therefore, (L) is the correct answer.

3. (A)

   Since $x = 2$ and $y = 8$,

   $$\sqrt{xy} = \sqrt{2(8)} = \sqrt{16} = 4$$

   Therefore, (A) is the correct answer.

4. (M)

   $100 = 10^2$, $400 = 20^2$, $900 = 30^2$, and $1600 = 40^2$. The equation best represents the relationship between the length and price of the material is $P = L^2$. Therefore, (M) is the correct answer.

5. (C)

   Twice the number of apples, A, can be written as $2A$. Thus, the number of oranges, O, is twenty more than twice the number of apples, A, is $O = 2A + 20$. Therefore, (C) is the correct answer.

6. (K)

   The product of x and y is 20 means $xy = 20$. Since the table in (K) best represents the relationship, (K) is the correct answer.

7. (D)

   The table represents the relationship such as the output is one more than half the input. Thus, the output when input is 2 is $\frac{2}{2} + 1 = 2$. Therefore, (D) is the correct answer.

8. (J)

Use the distributive property: $a(b - c) = ab - ac$. Thus, $\frac{2}{3}(12 - 6) = \frac{2}{3}(12) - \frac{2}{3}(6)$. Therefore, (J) is the correct answer.

9. (B)

Substituting $x = -1$ into $y = -x$ gives $y = -(-1) = 1$, which means that the ordered pair $(-1, 1)$ is on the line $y = -x$. Therefore, (B) is the correct answer.

10. (K)

The slope of a line $y = mx + b$ is m, the coefficient of x. The larger the m, the steeper the line is. Among the answer choices, 5 is the greatest coefficient of x. Therefore, (K) is the correct answer.

11. (D)

The cost of renting a bus is $\$k$. Since the cost is equally distributed among 10 students, the amount that each student pay is $\frac{\$k}{10}$. Therefore, (D) is the correct answer.

12. (L)

Since 1 yard is equal to 36 inches, 2 yards is equal to $2 \times 36 = 72$ inches, and X yards is equal to $X \times 36$ inches. Thus, $Y = 36X$. Therefore, (L) is the correct answer.

13. (C)

25% is equal to $\frac{1}{4}$. The price of a shirt, y, is 25% of the price of a jacket, x, can be written as $y = \frac{1}{4}x$. Since the table in (C) satisfies $y = \frac{1}{4}x$, (C) is the correct answer.

14. (L)

The table contains three ordered pairs: $(6, 0), (8, -2)$, and $(10, -4)$. The three ordered pairs satisfy the equation $y = -x + 6$ in (L). Therefore, (L) is the correct answer.

15. (C)

Substituting $x = 0$ into $y = -3x + 2$ gives $y = -3(0) + 2 = 2$. It means that the ordered pair $(0, 2)$ satisfies $y = -3x + 2$. Therefore, (C) is the correct answer.

Answers and Solutions

IAAT Practice Test 6 Section 4

Answers

1. B	2. M	3. D	4. M	5. A
6. J	7. C	8. L	9. A	10. J
11. D	12. L	13. B	14. M	15. B

Solutions

1. (B)

   Cross multiplying $\dfrac{x}{5} = \dfrac{3}{5}$ gives $5x = 15$. Thus, $x = 3$. Therefore, (B) is the correct answer.

2. (M)

   Use the distributive property: $-x(x + y) = -x \cdot x + -x \cdot y = -x^2 - xy$. Therefore, (M) is the correct answer.

3. (D)

   Since $x = 2$ and $y = -3$,

   (A) $x - y = 2 - (-3) = 5$

   (B) $-x + y = -2 + -3 = -5$

   (C) $-xy = -(2)(-3) = 6$

   (D) $2xy = 2(2)(-3) = -12$

   Therefore, the expression in (D) has the smallest value.

4. (M)

   Adding 7 to both sides of equation $2x - y - 7 = 0$ gives $2x - y = 7$. Therefore, the value of $2x - y$ is 7.

5. (A)

   Since $a \spadesuit b = \dfrac{b - a}{a + b}$,

   $$-2 \spadesuit 4 = \frac{4 - (-2)}{-2 + 4} = \frac{6}{2} = 3$$

   Therefore, (A) is the correct answer.

6. (J)

$$-x + 3 < 2$$
$$-x < -1$$
$$x > 1$$

Among the answer choices, only value that satisfies $x > 1$ is 2. Therefore, (J) is the correct answer.

7. (C)

Jason can wash $\frac{n}{2}$ cars in 1 hours, he can wash $6 \times \frac{n}{2} = 3n$ in 6 hours.

8. (L)

The volume of the cone with a height of 9 and a radius of 2 is

$$V = \frac{1}{3}\pi r^2 h = \frac{1}{3}\pi(2)^2(9) = 12\pi$$

Therefore, (L) is the correct answer.

9. (A)

$$2x - y - z + y = 2x + y - y - z = 2x - z$$

Therefore, (A) is the correct answer.

10. (J)

0 is greater than -2. Therefore, (J) is the correct answer.

11. (D)

The surface area of the cube with side length of 6 is $A = 6x^2 = 6(6)^2 = 216$. Therefore, (D) is the correct answer.

12. (L)

Since $2(4 + 3) = 14$, (L) is the correct answer.

13. (B)

$\frac{4}{x} + 1$ means that one more than the quotient of four and a number, x. Therefore, (B) is the correct answer.

14. (M)

The perimeter of the square is 16 implies that the length of the square is 4. Since the length of the square is increased by 2, the length of a new square is 6. Thus, the perimeter of the new square is $6 \times 4 = 24$. Therefore, (M) is the correct answer.

15. (B)

Since $e(x)$ be the sum of all even numbers less than or equal to x, $e(11) = 2 + 4 + 6 + 8 + 10 = 30$. Therefore, (B) is the correct answer.